The Shining Of Light

A History of the Wesley Foundation
at
The University of Tennessee,
Knoxville

1922-2007

Robert E. Parrott

TENNESSEE VALLEY
Publishing
2008

Copyright © 2007 Robert E. Parrott

Printed and bound in the United States of America. All rights reserved. No part of this book may be reproduced in any form or by any electronic or mechanical means including information storage and retrieval systems without permission in writing from the author except by a reviewer who may quote brief passages in a review.

Published by:

> Tennessee Valley Publishing,
> P.O. Box 52527,
> Knoxville, Tennessee 37950-2527
> www.TVP1.com

Library of Congress Control Number: 2008112371

ISBN-10: 1-932604-54-5

ISBN-13: 978-1-932604-54-2

Contents

List of Photographs iv

Author's Note vi

Foreword: "The Light Must Shine" ix

Chapter I   Beginnings (1922-1942) 1

Chapter II   The McDonough Years (1942-1951) 9

Chapter III   Last Days on Temple Avenue (1951-1956) 27

Chapter IV   Melrose Place (1956-1960) 39

Chapter V   The Winds of Change (1960-1964) 55

Chapter VI   Bricks and Mortar (1964-1967) 75

Chapter VII   Being the Church (1967-1977) 91

Chapter VIII Stars Over Santa Cruz Mixtepec (1977-1982) .. 111

Chapter IX   Go Forth Believing (1982-1993) 131

Chapter X   A New Day (1993-2002) 159

Chapter XI   In A New World (2002-2007) 185

Afterword   "Take The Light With You" 201

Sources 205

List of Photographs

Cover photograph by Brandon Wright .... Front cover
International Student Dinner, 1990 viii
Church Street Methodist Church, ca 1922
    [McClung Collection] 8
Irvin and Evelyn McDonough 10
908 Temple Avenue, Knoxville 15
A Weekly Fireside, late 1940s 17
The Methodist Student Center 22
Relaxing at cards on Temple Avenue 23
A Circle of Friends 26
Glen Otis Martin 28
Meditation Chapel on Temple Avenue 31
On Retreat, early 1950s 33
Playing hobo on Temple Avenue 35
Entrance to the Meditation Chapel 38
The Old Wesley Foundation House 43
Fred Delap, Shirley Delap and Glen O. Martin 50
On Retreat, late 1950s 51
Chapel Ground Breaking, 1957, J.P. Hess, R.H. Duncan
    Charles Barber, George Smith, Martha Corey,
    Betty Patterson, Glen O. Martin, Lynn Testerman,
    Herbert L. Lee, and Sam Sims 54
George S. Paris, Myrtle Godwin, and James Clemmer 56
Working in the Melrose Place kitchen 61
Spring Banquet, 1961--Norma Dean Smith, soloist;
    James Clemmer, pianist 62
Sunday supper, early 1960s 66
Bible Study 74
Bob Parrott, 1964 76
Ground breaking, October 30, 1966 86
905 Mountcastle Street, Knoxville, Kenton Dickerson 87
The new building opens, September 23, 1967 89
Almost Finished 90
Theatre worship, ca 1968 92

List of Photographs (Continued)

'Bridges,' Bryan K. Crow, photographer	106
On Retreat at Camp Wesley Woods	107
Bright and Shining	109
Candle Lighting	110
Stars Over Santa Cruz Mixtepec, 1977-1982	118
Digging a latrine, 1979	119
The village fiesta, 1979	121
Godspell, 1980	126
Seasons: A Celebration of Life, 1982	129
Project Together, 1986	135
Deane Young and Kim Holden	136
Rafting on the Nantahala	138
Bill Hunt and the WHAM kids, 1989 Hallowe'en Party	146
Camelot, 1991	150
Guys and Dolls, 1992	155
Wedding of Cheryl Mobley and Alan Cloar; Enoch Hendry, officiating, 1994	161
At work on the Mexican mission, 1996	166
Mission work, Miguel Aleman, Mexico	167
B.J. McCullough and the WHAM kids, 1996	168
'CROP WALK,' 1997	170
Arsenic and Old Lace, 1997	171
The Importance of Being Earnest, 1998	174
The cast of *The Cotton Patch Gospel*, 1999	176
Wesleyan Heritage Trip, Savannah, GA, 1997	184
Lauri Jo Cranford	186
The Wesley Foundation Chapel	191
David Jackson	192
Wednesday night discussion group, 2007	197
On Melrose Place	200
Light!	203
Godspell, 1980	204

Author's Note

In 1947, I became active in a Wesley Foundation as a 16-year-old college freshman in Louisiana. At that time, the Louisiana Methodist Student Movement, which reflected the rising energy and the issues of the national Methodist Student Movement, was an exhilarating network, involving ten or more campuses. The annual Louisiana MSM Spring Conference and participation in MSM South Central Regional Training Conferences were highlights of the year for many students in the late 1940s, including myself. The MSM sounded a call to commitment and discipleship. It was in the challenging world of the Student Movement that campus ministry became the vocational goal of my life.

By 1954, after I had graduated from Perkins School of Theology at Southern Methodist University two years earlier, I was serving (at age 23) as the campus minister of the Wesley Foundation at Southwestern Louisiana Institute (a state college which then became the University of Southwestern Louisiana in Lafayette, now The University of Louisiana at Lafayette, home of the 'Ragin' Cajuns.') At a "Student Workers' Conference" in Nashville, I first became acquainted with Dr. Harvey C. Brown, then one of the two executive secretaries of the Department of College and University Religious Life (a division of the Methodist Board of Education), who was proudly identified as having established the Wesley Foundation at the University of Tennessee, Knoxville, "the oldest Wesley Foundation in the South." Following in the footsteps of John Wesley, Dr. Brown was one of the founding fathers of the Methodist ministry to college and university students.

Following the Supreme Court decision (*Brown v. Board of Education*) in spring 1954, the Lafayette campus of 5000 students rightly and immediately prepared to receive its first African-American students in the fall. Since classes began there in mid-

August, the campus was (in terms of the calendar) the first tax-supported collegiate institution in the Deep South to experience desegregation, and the Wesley Foundation excitedly opened its facilities and its program to *all* students. The experience confronted us with problems, including the anger of some District churches, the loss of District financial support and demands that the young campus minister be immediately removed. By May 1955, supported by courageous local clergy and laypeople, the Wesley Foundation had effected a smooth transition into a fully desegregated ministry. In early June, Dr. Brown made a trip from Nashville to Lafayette to commend the Wesley Foundation community and to celebrate what had been accomplished. He was a genial, fatherly figure known for his interesting anecdotes. He said to me, "You've made deep tracks in this place!" I will always remember that conversation.

Later that same summer (1955) I traveled by Trailways bus from Lafayette with a large group of students from the Louisiana MSM to Lake Junaluska, North Carolina to a Southeast Regional MSM Training Conference, and it was there that I first met students from the Wesley Foundation in nearby Knoxville. I was impressed with their articulateness and with their positive descriptions of the Knoxville program as well as their director Glen Otis Martin. In the course of attending both MSM and ecumenical conferences in the late 1950s, I became acquainted with George S. Paris, then soon to be the campus minister at the UTK Wesley Foundation. Like many others, I appreciated his engaging manner and his many abilities. Then, when I first arrived in Knoxville in June 1964, I met people who with deep appreciation remembered the work of J. Irvin McDonough. The McDonough influence is still present in the campus ministry, 65 years after he began his work here.

Unlike Harvey C. Brown, many people in positions of Methodist leadership were not encouraging to young clergy interested in campus ministry in the later 1940s, the 1950s and the early 1960s. Like others, I was often asked disparagingly when I was going to leave *student work* and enter *the ministry*. A bishop even suggested that he thought I was making a "serious professional mistake" by continuing in campus ministry as a vocational commitment. "You'll never get *anywhere* if you stay in campus ministry," he said.

Campus ministry as a life's work has been the wisest, most fulfilling professional choice I ever made.

Robert E. Parrott
December 2007

International Student Dinner, 1990

Foreword

"The Light Must Shine"

In late summer 1965, in the old house at 1718 Melrose Place in Knoxville, several meetings of the Building Committee of the Wesley Foundation Board of Directors were conducted in the living room, with the massive front door open to the night air because of the oppressive heat inside. The first-floor windows were stuck and could no longer be opened. There was excitement about the prospect of a new building to be built on this same site, but there was also an air of sadness about the coming demise of the old structure. The purpose of the meetings had been to discuss specific recommendations to be submitted to the architects, for plans and drawings were about to begin – recommendations about the building's appearance, its façade, its placement on the sharply inclined Melrose lot, its connection to the existing Chapel, its architectural style, and the message that the building would announce to the campus. In the last of these meetings, the Building Committee was particularly concerned about the *appearance* of the new structure to rise like a phoenix from the razing of the old.

J. Preston Hess, the venerable secretary of the University's Board of Trustees and an active layman at Church Street Methodist Church, was the chairperson of the Building Committee. A 1917 graduate of the University, he possessed a remarkable archive of information about the history of the campus and the history of the Wesley Foundation, and in his courtly manner, was able to penetrate to the heart of any discussion or to the core of any problem. On that humid summer evening, Mr. Hess reminisced briefly about the Foundation's history, especially the acquisition of the first Center building on Temple Avenue, and then shifted to the heart of the issue -- the new building's architectural image. The building should represent the Methodist Church, he said, and should be an expression of the love of God. After a discussion about the façade, he finally said, *"The light must shine from this place! It must be a shining light to the campus!"*

Although the phraseology of light had not been used in this exact manner previously in the committee meetings, the image and message of *light* had been basic to the Committee's work, for it was clear that the building and its ministry should boldly declare faith, knowledge and mission. Mr. Hess had rightly worded the idea as no one else had done. *The Wesley Foundation must be a shining light.*

The evening meeting had grown long. By unanimous agreement, the secretary of the Building Committee was requested to include this imagery of light in the conclusion of its written statement to the architects, for all were agreed – the building should *offer light,* the building should *project light*, the building should *share light*, the building should *say light*.

Mr. Hess offered a final prayer. Recommendations to the architects were concluded. The work of the Committee was finished. **The Light Must Shine**.

Chapter I

BEGINNINGS
(1922-1942)

1

People called Methodists were first identified on a university campus. In the late 1720s, in the secular environment of the Age of Enlightenment, Anglican John Wesley and his brother Charles gathered fellow students together for Bible study, prayer, spiritual self-examination, personal discipline and local missionary work in the jails adjacent to England's Oxford University. The Wesley brothers termed their organizational gatherings "The Holy Club." Almost two hundred years later, in 1913, Methodist Bishop James C. Baker established the first *Wesley Foundation* on the Urbana campus of the University of Illinois as a pioneer project of the Methodist Episcopal Church. The stated purpose of the new effort was to minister to college and university students on the state-supported campus, signifying Methodists' concern for those engaged in the pursuit of public education.

Trinity Methodist Church in Urbana, Illinois provided the home base for the development of this new experiment; in later years, Trinity *became* the Wesley Foundation for the Urbana campus – Trinity's dominant mission was focused on campus ministry. Bishop Baker's purposes included the provision of worship, religious education, leadership development for the Methodist Episcopal Church, and active recruitment for "full-time Christian vocations." The immediate result of the project was to provide "a home away from home" for students, particularly those whose permanent homes were elsewhere. He later reflected that he

THE SHINING OF LIGHT: A HISTORY OF THE WESLEY FOUNDATION AT THE UNIVERSITY OF TENNESSEE, 1922-2007

wanted to offer the same spiritual foundation to Methodist students at the University of Illinois that were then offered to students at church-related campuses.

Bishop Baker considered using the term "Holy Club" for the new movement, but decided that the pietist name would be considered dated and inappropriate in the second decade of the 20th century. He chose the term *Wesley Foundation* with the comment, ".....Let us build under the lives of these college youth a spiritual foundation such as John Wesley had after his Aldersgate experience." In this context, it has often been noted that John Wesley at work in Oxford University was the first Methodist "campus minister."

Less than ten years after the beginning of Bishop Baker's work on the Urbana campus of the University of Illinois, a Wesley Foundation nucleus was begun in Knoxville, Tennessee in 1922 as an evening fellowship group (sometimes described as a "Senior Epworth League") in Church Street Methodist Church. The meetings were held in the Church's elaborate Gothic Revival structure then located at 415 W. Church Street, across the street from the present-day Lawson McGhee Public Library. The purpose of the fellowship group was to minister to students attending the nearby University of Tennessee campus, especially to those who were "away from home." This Tennessee beginning was the first effort of campus ministry on a state-supported campus in the Southeastern region of the Methodist Episcopal Church, South. Even more significantly, it was the beginning of a Wesley Foundation in the first non-sectarian college chartered in the United States -- for the University of Tennessee, begun as tiny Blount College in 1797, had been authorized by the nation's first territorial legislature meeting in Knoxville in 1794.

In the wake of the Knoxville experiment, other campuses in the Southeast soon organized nucleus groups which became

BEGINNINGS
(1922-1942)

Wesley Foundations – the University of Alabama in 1923, the University of Florida and the University of Mississippi in 1924, the University of North Carolina in 1925, Florida State College for Women in 1926, and the University of Georgia in 1927. The financial constraints of the Depression in the 1930s curtailed the development of campus ministries (and in some cases, forced their abandonment for almost a decade), but by 1939, when the Methodist Episcopal Church and the Methodist Episcopal Church, South (which had been divided since 1844 because of the slavery issue), were reunited as The Methodist Church, church-wide interest in "student work" (as campus ministry was then usually termed) had increased with the formation of a national-level Methodist Student Movement (MSM).

2

At the time of the Wesley Foundation's founding in Knoxville, the university campus was relatively small, still clustered in brick and frame buildings primarily on The Hill, newly centered by Ayres Hall built the year before, in 1921. On Cumberland Avenue, where Hoskins Library is now located, stood the imposing Victorian mansion belonging to the Woodruff family. The University had recently purchased and torn down the elaborate Cowan-Briscoe house, and would shortly build Sophronia Strong Residence Hall on the same site. The College of Agriculture had its own separate location west of the Hill within sight of Kingston Pike, the primary two-lane highway which led to Nashville. In 1922, Kingston Pike was unpaved after it passed the Agriculture campus.

In 1922, the pastor of Church Street Methodist Church was Forest J. Prettyman. W.L. Lyons was chairman of the Board of Stewards and W.B. Sullins was treasurer, while J.S. French was the Knoxville District presiding elder. The total church membership was 1226; the total value of the church property was

THE SHINING OF LIGHT: A HISTORY OF THE WESLEY FOUNDATION AT THE UNIVERSITY OF TENNESSEE, 1922-2007

$125,000. The well-known evangelist Billy Sunday held an evangelistic campaign in Knoxville in 1922, to which Church Street members contributed a total of $1000. One of the first indications of the organization of a specific university "student program" was entered in the minutes of the Board of Stewards on September 11, 1922, reporting on a discussion to secure a "Secretary for the University Work." In that year, the Church Street Methodist Epworth League (forerunner of the Methodist Youth Fellowship and United Methodist Youth Fellowship) reported a combined total of 102 members, perhaps indicating both a high-school level League and a university-level League.

In 1924, Percy R. Knickerbocker was appointed pastor of Church Street Methodist Church, followed by C.C. Grimes, W.R. Hendrix, W.F. Blackard and J.A. Bays. From its inception, the Wesley Foundation was perceived by the pastors and by the congregation of Church Street Methodist Church as a local means by which to serve the Methodist student constituency of the University. However, the total thrust of the congregation did not become *the* Wesley Foundation, as was true at Trinity Methodist Church in Urbana.

A disastrous fire in 1928 destroyed Church Street Methodist's buildings on Church Street, and the decision to build a new Gothic-style church at Mecklenburg Place on the corner of Henley Street and Cumberland Avenue (Main Street) resulted in a change of location – within sight of the University – while retaining the traditional name "Church Street Methodist Church." The construction of the new church building on the new site (near the corner where the East Tennessee Female Institute had educated women students from 1828 to 1893) was one of the city's few major building projects undertaken during 1929-1930, the earliest Depression years.

BEGINNINGS
(1922-1942)

During the 1920s, the task of leadership of the Wesley Foundation (then still only a "co-ed" Sunday School class meeting at 9:15 a.m. and an evening student fellowship activity) was assigned to Church Street Methodist staff members. The first remembered or recorded assistant pastor with this responsibility was J. Earl Gilbreath, who was appointed on October 21, 1924. He remained in the position until January 10, 1926, when he was moved to Broad Street Methodist Church in Kingsport, TN. Following Earl Gilbreath as assistant pastor (in 1926) was Harvey C. Brown, who had held pastorates in Alabama where he was remembered as doing "special work with young people." One of the first notations of his distinguished tenure at Church Street Methodist was the fact that he was furnished a typewriter. Harvey C. Brown, a graduate of Emory University and Drew Theological Seminary, can rightly be termed the father of the UTK Wesley Foundation; his indelible stamp on the ministry to the university can still be felt. In his later capacity as executive secretary of the Methodist Church's Department of College and University Religious Life, a division of the General Board of Higher Education with offices in Nashville, TN, he often commended individual "student workers" when they left "deep tracks" on a campus. By the time he left his position as Church Street Methodist's assistant pastor in 1933, Harvey C. Brown had left his own "deep tracks" on the UTK campus.

In the files of Church Street Methodist Church there remains a yellowed newspaper advertisement (dating from 1926 or 1927) announcing that, in the Sunday absence of Dr. Knickerbocker, "Rev. Harvey C. Brown, University Pastor" was to preach on the sermon topic, "Jesus Our Supreme Consideration," giving "concrete instances of the power of religion and of the reality of Christ to resurrect men from dead lives." The same advertisement welcomed university students to Sunday morning church services, saying "You are perhaps far from home, but you are most welcome here." The student fellowship meeting began

THE SHINING OF LIGHT: A HISTORY OF THE WESLEY FOUNDATION
AT THE UNIVERSITY OF TENNESSEE, 1922-2007

Sunday evening activities with supper at 5:45 p.m. and devotions at 6:30 p.m. The announcement concluded with the invitation, "…..We are eager to have University students with us."

On the evening of February 19, 1928, when fire in the church was discovered (in the ceiling beams) at the conclusion of the Sunday evening service, it was often remembered that Assistant Pastor Harvey C. Brown was about to offer the benediction. A member of the congregation rose and announced that the church was on fire, and urged everyone to exit the sanctuary rapidly. Whether Harvey Brown actually pronounced a hurried benediction was not recorded.

Much of Harvey Brown's work was then diverted to the long process of assisting with the Church's temporary relocation and plans for the building of the new church structure. On April 1, 1930, a publication entitled The Church Letter (Vol. I, #2) stated that the projected cost of the "new Plant" was to be $637,479, and that the church staff consisted of pastor C.C. Grimes, assistant pastor Harvey C. Brown, and "Miss Myrtle Long, Sec'y."

By 1933, when Harvey C. Brown accepted another position and left Church Street Methodist, the deepening Depression and the debt incurred by the construction of the new building severely limited and then forced the discontinuance of the financial resources which could be invested into the development of a campus ministry. Little more than a Sunday School class for university students was maintained. On October 13, 1936, the Board of Stewards minutes noted that a "senior student" was to be asked to do "the work of the Church at the University of Tennessee instead of the Assistant Pastor."

At the time of the Wesley Foundation's first organization as a fellowship group, Dr. Harcourt A. Morgan, an active layman at Church Street Methodist Church, was president of the University

BEGINNINGS
(1922-1942)

of Tennessee. Dr. Morgan fully supported the idea of a specialized ministry to university students. Four years before his death, he presented a wooden cross to the Foundation, on which was attached a brass plaque inscribed *Presented to the Wesley Foundation by H.A. Morgan, 1946.* He also bequeathed one of his personal Bibles to the small library owned by the Wesley Foundation, as well as a book published in 1890, *From Epworth to London with John Wesley: Being Fifty Photo-Engravings of the Sacred Places of Methodism,* by George John Stevenson.

By 1942, the new Methodist Student Movement, organized six years earlier at a student conference in St. Louis, MO, had slowly begun to create its own identity as a national and international network of issues and ideas of interest to college and university students. It successfully began to connect Methodist students to the larger world, especially in the dark days of the later 1930s and through the years of World War II. During the 1950s and the turbulent early 1960s, the MSM was to become – in the lives of generations of students -- a profound growth experience as well as a rallying cry for social change.

THE SHINING OF LIGHT: A HISTORY OF THE WESLEY FOUNDATION
AT THE UNIVERSITY OF TENNESSEE, 1922-2007

Church Street Methodist Church, ca 1922 [McClung Collection]

Chapter II

THE McDONOUGH YEARS
(1942-1951)

1

On September 1, 1942, James Irvin McDonough arrived in Knoxville, appointed by Holston Conference Bishop Paul B. Kern to become the first full-time campus minister of the UTK Wesley Foundation; officially, he was described as the "Director of the Wesley Foundation" or the "University of Tennessee Student Worker." Earlier in his career he had served pastorates in Middle Tennessee, and since 1939, he had served as chaplain and instructor of Bible at Hiwassee College in Madisonville, TN. Affectionately known as "Mr. Mack," he and his wife Evelyn McDonough ("Mrs. Mack") were faced with the task of organizing and giving shape to the new "student ministry" on The Hill, working from a base at Church Street Methodist Church. The McDonoughs were introduced to the congregation of the church on their first Sunday in Knoxville by the new senior pastor, Dr. James Alexander (Alex) Bays, who had been appointed there a short time previously. The arrival of J. Irvin McDonough and J.A. Bays in the same year marked a significant turning point for the Foundation's future, for Dr. Bays had already lent his considerable support to the dream of a student ministry with a presence "on campus" and an eventual center of its own.

Irvin McDonough's beginning yearly salary was $3000. Although he was a duly appointed Methodist clergyman, no provision was made to supply him a parsonage. He was probably given a small housing allowance. At first the McDonoughs lived in an apartment on Cumberland Avenue, and then occupied a house in North Knoxville until the first Center building was acquired in 1943.

Irvin and Evelyn McDonough

Other people at Church Street Methodist Church involved in this new effort included Frank and Ruth DeFriese, J. Preston Hess, Lola Acuff, Mr. and Mrs. Pat Murphy and Mrs. Arthur Peterson. At Knoxville's First Methodist Church (formerly a Methodist Episcopal Church) located a few blocks away from Church Street Methodist, Dr. Neal Dow Peacock, a faculty member in the College of Agriculture, also gave his unreserved support. These early heroes of the UTK Wesley Foundation followed in the footsteps of Harvey C. Brown, and – with J. Irvin and Evelyn McDonough, and Dr. Alex Bays -- made their own deep tracks. The Wesley Foundation could not have developed without their vision and hard work.

Important to Mr. Mack's efforts was the cooperation of the University administration and the Knoxville District churches. Through the assistance of Ralph W. Frost, then the local General Secretary of the Young Men's Christian Association (known at UTK as "The Christian Associations"), the University provided the Methodist group with office space in the three-story brick "Y" Building. Opened in 1891, located where Hesler Hall stands today,

THE McDONOUGH YEARS
(1942-1951)

the building contained a two-story gymnasium with an oval track at the balcony level, a small swimming pool, a bowling alley, a reading room, an assembly hall, a snack shop and dormitory rooms. The world-wide YMCA movement had begun in London in 1844 as an evangelical effort intended to minister to young working men, and it consequently founded pioneer chapters in both the University of Michigan and the University of Virginia as early as 1858, followed in later years by YMCA chapters on a multitude of American campuses throughout the nation, seeking to relate the Christian life to the experience of a university education. In its early glory days at UTK, the YMCA had sponsored Bible study and mandatory chapel services, but later developed programs with a wider appeal to the campus – Freshman Vespers, Thanksgiving and Easter services, a mid-winter Convocation, and the Aloha Oe ritual for graduating seniors.

By the mid-1930s, the YMCA's vital campus function had begun to lose its vigorous, turn-of-the-century appeal, but the "Y" Building continued to function as the campus student center in many of the same ways in which the Carolyn P. Brown University Center, built in 1954, does today. Because of the strategic location of The Christian Associations' building, the new Wesley Foundation office functioned in the heart of the campus. A significant outgrowth of the YMCA was the establishment (in 1928) of the Tennessee School of Religion by several leading Knoxville Protestant churches, through which UTK students could take elective credit courses in Biblical study and theology, taught by qualified local clergy. Mr. Mack was the first of the Wesley Foundation directors to teach in the Tennessee School of Religion, in a system which later also included the Baptist, Presbyterian and Roman Catholic campus ministers. Subsequent Wesley Foundation directors who were also members of this faculty were Glen Otis Martin, George S. Paris and Robert E. Parrott.

THE SHINING OF LIGHT: A HISTORY OF THE WESLEY FOUNDATION AT THE UNIVERSITY OF TENNESSEE, 1922-2007

Donations (and loaned items) from Methodist churches and individuals in Knoxville provided furnishings and equipment for the first Wesley Foundation office which was to serve as the on-campus headquarters. Alumni later remembered that among the furnishings were a wooden desk and desk chair, a file cabinet, a bookcase, a typewriter and two "easy chairs." It was there that the first Wesley Foundation program was planned during the fall quarter 1942, where the first official contacts with in-coming students were made and the first officers of a Student Council were elected. By this time, the December 7, 1941 attack on Pearl Harbor and the entrance of the United States into World War II had radically altered the UTK campus, especially since the number of male students was greatly reduced and the first full effects of the local "war effort" were experienced.

A Board of Directors for the Wesley Foundation was formed, charged with the responsibility of guiding the development and financing of the organization, its first membership including J.A. Bays, J. Preston Hess, architect Charles Barber, George H. Smith, Neal D. Peacock, and U.S. Senator William Emerson Brock of Chattanooga (founder of the Brock Candy Company). Although not a member of the Board, Bishop Kern served as a consultant and advisor, as did Bishop Marvin Franklin of the Mississippi Area. One early decision of the Board directed that no Methodist student activity would be conducted "on the Hill" during Church Street Methodist Church's scheduled services.

On February 8, 1943, an early morning fire (caused by an overheated electric motor in the basement) complctcly destroyed the 52-year-old "Y" building, including all the furnishings, books, records, office equipment and supplies of the Wesley Foundation. Once again the University came to the Foundation's assistance, and temporary office space (for a few months) was provided on the third floor of the newly built Biology Building, apparently in

THE McDONOUGH YEARS
(1942-1951)

conjunction with office space allocated to the Tennessee School of Religion. Here the Wesley Foundation office continued – with furniture and a typewriter loaned by the University – until fall 1943.

2

Long before the fire at the "Y" Building, it had become apparent that the Wesley Foundation needed a Center – a "gathering place" and a separate on-campus identity of its own – if the young movement to serve Methodist students was to grow and flourish. A petition, organized by J.A. Bays and others, bearing the names of hundreds of Methodists, was presented to Bishop Kern and to the memberships of the three Tennessee Annual Conferences (Holston, Tennessee, Memphis) requesting a separate building. The petition and the movement were heartily supported by Bishop Kern, and funds were raised ("in nickels and dimes," it was said) for the new beginning. By early 1943, the amount of $1500 (an enormous sum in the post-Depression years) had been raised. (The vital roles played by Dr. Bays and Bishop Kern in the official launching of the UTK Wesley Foundation into a separate building were highlighted for many years by their framed photographs which hung in prominent places at 908 Temple Avenue and 1718 Melrose Place.)

By 1943, Associate Pastor Marvin Franklin, Jr. (the son of Bishop Franklin) was appointed to Church Street Methodist Church, and he became another ardent supporter of the Wesley Foundation effort – and popular with University students. A former captain of the Vanderbilt University football team, he had just been released from military service, and since there was at that time no available housing in Knoxville for his wife and daughter, he lived temporarily with the DeFriese family. Another Associate Pastor, Wilson Elliott, also became closely associated with the Wesley Foundation community.

13

THE SHINING OF LIGHT: A HISTORY OF THE WESLEY FOUNDATION
AT THE UNIVERSITY OF TENNESSEE, 1922-2007

Dr. Bays headed a committee to select and negotiate the purchase of an appropriate house or building which could be converted into a "Methodist Student Center." In January 1943, negotiations were begun for the purchase of the residence of real estate executive Benjamin H. Sprankle at 908 Temple Avenue, a site now occupied by the Claxton Education Building. The street is now named Volunteer Boulevard. The Sprankles were a leading Knoxville family who had purchased the house from U.D. and Bessie Beeler in 1924; the Sprankles' original real estate office at 428 Union Street still remains as a structure of historic importance in Knoxville. In 1943, Temple Avenue was a well-known address, for the residence of UTK President James D. Hoskins was located nearby (at #834), and the families of W.M. Burkhardt and E.T. Bowman were next-door neighbors. At #917, in the rear of the McGhee residence, was located Miss Annie McGhee's Dancing Studio. Across the street from the Sprankle residence (at #949), was the imposing home of the W.J. McClure family – the site is now occupied by the McClung Tower. At the corner of Temple and Melrose Place was the huge Shields residence, later to become the UTK Faculty Club which provided accommodations for single UTK faculty men on the upper floors.

By May 1943 an agreement had been reached concerning the purchase price for the Sprankle house, and Senator Brock of Chattanooga agreed to serve as the leader of a fund solicitation campaign for the direct purchase. In addition to Senator Brock's financial campaign within the Holston Conference, the Tennessee and Memphis Conferences also raised money for acquiring the building, and approximately $500 was received from each of these Conferences. At the end of the campaigns, it was reported that the building had been secured for a total cost of $24,000. When building debts were finally paid, there was reputedly 24 cents remaining in the Wesley Foundation's bank account.

THE McDONOUGH YEARS
(1942-1951)

Methodist Student Center, University of Tennessee, 908 Temple Avenue, Knoxville, Tennessee

908 Temple Avenue, Knoxville

The Sprankle house was a two-story brick residence of modified neo-Tudor style built circa 1915. On June 1, 1943, although few funds were available for the renovation and redecorating of the residence, work was begun in converting it to a serviceable Center. The "labor of love" (cleaning, painting, repair work, wall papering, floor refinishing, upholstering and drapery making) was done primarily by the McDonoughs, the DeFrieses and students. The first floor was organized with a living room, a dining room, a reading room, a sun room and a kitchen. Mr. Mack's office was also on the first floor. The second floor was converted into an apartment for the director and his family. One room in the basement was furnished for occupancy by two male UTK students, who tended the furnace and mowed the grass. Another section of the basement was later developed into a recreation room.

THE SHINING OF LIGHT: A HISTORY OF THE WESLEY FOUNDATION
AT THE UNIVERSITY OF TENNESSEE, 1922-2007

The new Center became a "home-away-from-home" for many students, echoing a part of Bishop Baker's original concept. This widespread idea of a comfortable "home," although severely criticized within a few years as "hand-holding" and the dispensing of "tea and cookies" to keep students from the "evils" of the university, represented a valid effort to provide a pleasant environment where students could *gather* and as a locus where ministry could be developed. The home-away-from-home approach received the approval of the University, and – despite its tendency to contain and confine ministry too tightly within a building, and to shield students from larger societal pressures – it offered a valid, exciting beginning point. The house at 908 Temple Avenue is still remembered as the first denominational Center on the UTK campus.

3

Despite the problems of launching the new ministry in the midst of wartime when rationing often necessitated unusual survival tactics, there began a highly successful period of development in the decade of the 1940s under the leadership of "Mr. Mack" and "Mrs. Mack." In the midst of the war years, Irvin and Evelyn McDonough created a warm, inviting atmosphere in the converted residence similar to an active community center, and here the revitalized ministry was truly launched as a full-time effort. The interior of the living room is recalled in 1940s photographs – striped living room wallpaper, comfortable wing chairs, and a square tiled fireplace topped by wall sconces and a gold-framed mirror. The dining room is also shown in a photograph as the setting for a formal reception, in which UTK women students, dressed in floor length formal attire, are served tea at a silver service by Ruth DeFriese. Standing in this group is Jean Martin Reese, wearing a large white corsage. A dark-stained staircase in the entrance hall was accented by large-patterned

THE McDONOUGH YEARS
(1942-1951)

wallpaper. Dark-stained doorways on the main floor had unusual peaked surrounds.

Contact was made with in-coming students through cooperation with the University's Freshman Week, and general monthly meetings of Methodist students were organized. A Student Council held regular sessions, for the principle of student involvement in program decision-making was paramount from the beginning, as a means of student leadership training. The role of students in decision-making and the willingness of the Board of Directors to respond to student ideas was a significant early theme, enlarged and deepened later during the mid-1960s and afterward.

An important event in the McDonough years and in the life of the Center was the birth of James Duggins (Dugg) McDonough. In later years, Dugg McDonough became the opera director first at Temple University in Philadelphia and then at L.S.U. in Baton Rouge.

Early features of the Wesley Foundation program at 908 Temple Avenue were twice-weekly Fireside Chats and Open

A weekly Fireside, late 1940s

THE SHINING OF LIGHT: A HISTORY OF THE WESLEY FOUNDATION AT THE UNIVERSITY OF TENNESSEE, 1922-2007

Houses, at which refreshments were served, usually prepared by Evelyn McDonough and Ruth DeFriese. Sunday School classes for University students continued at Church Street Methodist Church, taught by Alice Bays, Martha Holt, Lola Acuff, and Irvin McDonough. Sunday evening suppers at the church continued and increased in attendance, often with 100 students participating. There were quarterly weekend planning retreats, at first at the Kiwanis Fresh Air Camp on Prosser Road and there were retreats to Lake Junaluska, North Carolina, where Bishop Kern was remembered as grilling hamburgers in his back yard for the students.

As happened often in subsequent decades, many couples first met at the Wesley Foundation, and some were married there – in the living room at 908 Temple Avenue. Among those at whose marriage services Mr. Mack officiated were Mary Lois Quinton and Roy Godsey, Carol and Josh Brown, Jean Martin and Don Reese, and Dolores Allen and Frank N. Browder. Many of those married there long remembered their association with the McDonoughs and the DeFrieses. In February 1981, Dolores Allen Browder made a gift to one of the many fund-raising efforts of the Wesley Foundation. Responding to the this gift, Board president James Crook wrote to Ruth and Frank DeFriese, "A gift was received by the Wesley Foundation at the University of Tennessee toward our fund raising campaign from Dolores Allen Browder in your honor. This gift encourages a program which is growing in scope and size, and is greatly appreciated by this campus ministry. We are in great need of additional hymnals to be used in our ministry, and therefore would like to purchase these with this gift. Inside the new hymnals we will put bookplates indicating that they were given to the Wesley Foundation by Ms. Browder in honor of Mr. and Mrs. Frank DeFriese."

Few records of the day-by-day program details of the early years of the decade of the 1940s survive, but documentation which

THE McDONOUGH YEARS
(1942-1951)

has been maintained reveals an interesting look at the character of the campus. The elected president of the Wesley Foundation Student Council in 1944 was Howard Dale, from Hampshire, TN; other officers were Mary Meacham (Franklin, TN), Margaret Peacock (Knoxville), and Sara Jo Underwood (Livingstone, TN). Howard Dale's word of welcome to in-coming students in the earliest preserved brochure said, "…..A college education is a great step, perhaps the greatest, in preparation for the life one is to lead. No matter what route this preparation may take, a prerequisite for a truly great life in any field is a functioning knowledge of the Christian way of life." In the brochure, Mr. Mack announced his office hours: in the mornings he could be found in the office of The Tennessee School of Religion, Room 119, Biology Building, and in the afternoons he was available in his office at 908 Temple Avenue. Other early student participants in 1944-1945 included Patricia Trigg, Eleanor McCallum, Betty Jane Hicks, Blanche Myers, Sara Gardner, Lillian Davis, Corinne McDavid, Mary Johnston, Marion Carothers, Phyllis Wade, Ann James, Marile Edwards and Tupper Dooley.

A mimeographed report of the "Youth Division" of Church Street United Methodist Church for November 1945 indicates that Wesley Foundation activities included a Sunday School class (at the church) as well as Sunday evening discussions and a supper meal at 908 Temple Avenue; the discussion was led by a "principal speaker." There were also Thursday evening prayer services at the Center. Looking forward to the normalization of the student body following the War, it was noted in the Youth Division report that attendance was expected to increase when veterans returned from military service. At the time, the Church Street Methodist Church budget showed an item of $200 as financial support for the Wesley Foundation.

The academic year of 1946-1947 was marked by student leadership from Susan Swann of Mobile, Alabama; other officers were Agnes Callis, Marion Lyle and Burchard Jones. Committees noted included Membership and Attendance, Publicity, Recreation and Fellowship, World Friendship, Social Action, Dramatics and Music. A brochure produced in 1946 contains photographs of well-dressed students (men in dark suits, white shirts and ties, while women wore sweaters and skirts) likely gathered in a week-end conference setting, as well as students posed with a group of children, probably from the Dale Avenue Settlement House. Views of the interior of the house at 908 Temple Avenue show students playing table games, gathered singing around a piano, and paused (likely in the living room) for informal Devotions. Susan Swann's word of welcome to in-coming students said, "We hope you will want to take an active part in our program and we are looking forward to your being a member of our group. It is in college that we must choose the people, the organizations and the ideals that will give us a foundation for living for the rest of our lives."

In 1946-1947, the organized program included a "Gather-In" on Sunday evenings at 8:00 p.m. and mid-week worship at 7:00 p.m., followed by Council and committee meetings. There was "Chorus practice" on Friday nights at 7:00 p.m. In this year, Mr. Mack wrote of his goals for campus ministry, "Christianity has the universe on its side. This is our basic philosophy as we try to lead a student program at the University. As we discover the principles of Christianity in understanding and practice, we are assured that life in its fullness will unfold." Names of those recorded as "active" Wesley Foundationers in 1946-1947 were Tom Swift, Jean Bonner, Chester Campbell, Dorothy Troxler, Jean Martin, Russell Dynes, Carol Crosley, Mary Lois Quinton, Sarah Murphy, Kenneth Phifer, Dorothy Kerr, Mary Elizabeth Sartain, Mary Shadow, Virginia Callen and Marie Smith.

Large numbers of military veterans utilizing the G.I. Bill flooded the campus -- and university facilities were strained to keep pace with an increased student body and post-war needs. A

THE McDONOUGH YEARS
(1942-1951)

sense of new energy prevailed. The Wesley Foundation was reaching its full stride as a strong, protective, nurturing extension of the ministry of the Church. Many students of this generation remembered the Wesley Foundation as a haven, as a hub, as a welcoming "Home Away From Home." In this context, many Methodists across the state in the three Annual Conferences strongly encouraged their sons and daughters to seek out the Wesley Foundation when they entered the University. However, few parents or students likely realized the momentous changes which were soon to alter the character of collegiate life and the fabric of campus ministry.

The 1947-1948 school year included an emphasis on fellowship with international students, and a program by which a family in Poland (still suffering the ravages of life in post-war Europe) was adopted and supported financially by Wesley Foundation students. The president for that year was Claude Vance of Bristol, Tennessee; other officers were Joanne Smith, Alice Lyle and Ben Cockrill. Students set $200 as a goal for their combined personal contributions to the Foundation's budget -- by December 4, 1947, $175 had been pledged. Other activities included deputation teams, "dramatics," and work with Wesley House Community Center. There is evidence of participation in the State Student Christian Conference in Nashville. Listed topics for speakers at Wesley Foundation meetings included "Christian Symbolism," "Psychiatry and Mental Health" and "The Psychology of a Religious Experience."

A "Life Service Fellowship," in conjunction with other Christian organizations, was organized as a support system for those students interested in vocations within the Church. This group had its own elected officers, including Jack Caudill, Carolyn Elkins and Ewell Reagin. (In later years, Ewell Reagin was to be the campus minister of the Presbyterian Student Center on campus.) Other Life Service participants were Dave Klein, Ken Mills, Alice Lyle, Serill MacMurry, Benton Ellis and Don Moore.

The Methodist Student Center

In 1948-1949, the student president was Joe Peacock of Knoxville. (In later years, Joe became one of the Wesley Foundation directors at the University of Illinois.) Other officers were Alice Lyle, Jean Collier and Carroll Roberts. Handwritten minutes are extant in the Wesley Foundation files for Council meetings in spring 1949, noting that a Thursday "Fireside" had been added to the week's program, as well as drama, Holy Week services, a community service project at Pittman Center, and a "Candy Party" as a fund-raising event in support of Methodist World Service. There was also expanded work with children at the Dale Avenue Settlement House. The spring retreat was held at the Gatlinburg Assembly Grounds. Plans were made for sending delegates to a Regional Training Conference at Lake Junaluska in the summer of 1949. Other students assuming leadership roles were Ruth Ellen Kelly, Jo Motlow, Jack Krinckle, and Helen Gillenwater. The 1948-1949 introductory brochure proudly declared: "The Wesley Foundation is the national organization of

THE McDONOUGH YEARS
(1942-1951)

Methodist students. The 'Home' for Methodist students attending the University of Tennessee is the Methodist Student Center, 908 Temple Avenue. The Center is open each day from 8 a.m. until 10 p.m. It is for Foundation members and their friends to enjoy: the kitchen, the living room with piano and record player, the recreation rooms in the basement, and the backyard with furnace and outdoor games."

Relaxing at cards on Temple Avenue

The Wesley Foundation's Annual Banquet was held at the S. & W. Cafeteria on Gay Street, Knoxville on Saturday, March 26, 1949. (There had been considerable Council discussion about having the banquet at Church Street Methodist Church – at 50c per plate.) The Banquet's theme was declared to be "April Fun!" The toastmaster was Charles Ayres, and the "directors" were listed as "Mr. and Mrs. J.I. McDonough and 'Dugg'."

A set of typed notes exists for the Council's activities in 1949-1950, with Ben Cockrill serving as president, Ruth Ellen Kelly as vice-president, and Lora Jean Hinton, secretary. The students' budget for the year totaled $350, including $200 toward the upkeep of the "Wesley Foundation Center." Community work focused on Pittman Center (in Sevier County), Wesley House Community Center in Mechanicsville, and the Tarleton House for Boys. A major concern was continuing support for the Polish

THE SHINING OF LIGHT: A HISTORY OF THE WESLEY FOUNDATION
AT THE UNIVERSITY OF TENNESSEE, 1922-2007

family, to whom $32.00 was sent. In addition, a gift of $100 was given to "Mary, a foreign student from Japan" to enable her to come to the UTK campus to study. The Council for 1950-1951 was headed by Philip (Phil) Gates of Memphis, TN.

Retreats in the later 1940s and early 1950s are still recalled by Wesley Foundation students. These week-end "get-aways" from the schedules and busyness of campus life became highlights of a quarter's activities. Retreats were usually scheduled from Friday afternoons to Sundays in rural settings, often to places in the foothills of the Smoky Mountains. Late 1940s photographs still exist, showing excited students in retreat settings, enjoying mountain settings at Camp Montvale or Camp Wesley Woods. One photograph shows a collection of at least 12 students sitting crowded in the back of an open farm truck, while one student (Ruth Ellen Kelley of Memphis) stood precariously, holding on to the side of the truck. Ruth Ellen later received the Master of Christian Education degree from Perkins School of Theology, S.M.U., Dallas, Texas.

During the 1940s and early 1950s, the Foundation's program was largely local in character, and was understood as an expression and extension of the ministry of Church Street Methodist Church, other Knoxville churches and of the Knoxville District. However, significant national movements began to widen this focus. In Nashville, leadership from the Church's Department of College and University Religious Life (headed by Harvey C. Brown) was shaping new ways of thinking focused on more direct confrontation with the major issues of nation and world. With much vitality, many of these views were fashioned by the remnants of the Social Gospel movement of Walter Rauschenbusch, as well as the power of Post-Liberal theology. Increasingly Wesley Foundations were influenced by voices at the massive quadrennial conferences of the Methodist Student Movement held on Midwestern campuses (e.g., in Urbana, Illinois, Lincoln, Nebraska,

THE McDONOUGH YEARS
(1942-1951)

Topeka, Kansas and Lawrence, Kansas), to which student delegations from UTK were sent. The force of thousands of students gathered at these conferences – described as "gathered, challenged, inspired, motivated, confronted and empowered" -- made a profound impact on local campuses. The magazine *motive*, first published in 1941, became the voice of the Methodist Student Movement, and began to influence local programming, especially in its emphasis on the arts (poetry, literature, drama, music, film, and visual representation), as well as discussions on major theological and political issues by such leading thinkers as Reinhold and H. Richard Niebuhr, Albert Einstein and Paul Tillich.

The age of a new national student presence had begun. This shift in perspective clearly impacted the Knoxville Methodist student community. Change was in the air.

THE SHINING OF LIGHT: A HISTORY OF THE WESLEY FOUNDATION
AT THE UNIVERSITY OF TENNESSEE, 1922-2007

A Circle of Friends

Chapter III

LAST DAYS ON TEMPLE AVENUE
(1951-1956)

1

In early 1951, J. Irvin McDonough (the beloved "Mr. Mack") accepted a position as a member of the national staff of the Methodist Church's Board of Education with headquarters in Nashville. His new responsibilities included supervision of the certification of 8400 instructors who served annually in 1500 Methodist leadership training schools throughout the nation. After a highly successful ministry of eight and a half years at UTK, in which he touched the lives of an enormous number of students, he left a legacy which shaped the Wesley Foundation's ministry in significant ways for the years ahead. Students with whom he worked still continue after almost sixty years to remember the integrity and depth of his influence. By 1951, the pioneering "Knoxville unit" was considered one of the strongest Wesley Foundations in The Methodist Church.

While a new campus minister was being selected, Cecil P. Hardin, pastor of Church Street Methodist Church, served both as director of the Wesley Foundation and as dean of the Tennessee School of Religion.

In March 1951, a new director was appointed: Dr. Glen Otis Martin came to Knoxville from his position as Director of Religious Life at Hamline University in Minneapolis, Minnesota, bringing with him a gift for order, efficiency and program organization. The energetic Ph.D. scholar wore a flat-top hairstyle then becoming popular on campuses, and was called "Curly" by his friends. Curly Martin was to offer to the UTK Wesley Foundation another period of significant growth during his almost ten years as campus minister. Shortly after his arrival, Glen Martin was interviewed by a reporter from *The Knoxville News-Sentinel* who asked him what his plans were for the ministry of the Wesley Foundation. He answered that he had just arrived from Minneapolis, and was looking forward to meeting with the Foundation's students to discover what *their* ideas and aspirations were. The reply was a metaphor for much of his ministry, for he developed new and different ways in which students could be involved in program decision-making. Although different from the traditional, fatherly presence of Mr. Mack, Glen made a swift, impressive entrance into the life of the Wesley Foundation.

In addition to his intensive work at the 908 Temple Avenue Center, Glen Martin taught elective courses in "Bible and Religion" at the School of Religion, and soon reported that his "parish" consisted of more than 1300 Methodist students. Rapidly, the Foundation's program shifted to include more weekly Bible study, as well as more discussion programs, meals and an expansion of work at Wesley House Community Center. There were preaching and teaching missions to the churches of the Pittman Center Circuit (in the Smoky Mountains), where close relationships with these congregations were developed. For example, students soon donated several pints of blood to an elderly woman in one of these churches.

Glen Otis Martin

LAST DAYS ON TEMPLE AVENUE
(1951-1956)

In early fall 1952, Glen Martin wrote an article for *The Knoxville News-Sentinel,* entitled "Religion Encouraged on College Campuses: Wesley Foundation, at U-T and Universities Across Country, Is Function of Methodism." Accompanied by a large photograph of the house at 908 Temple Avenue, Glen offered his perspective on the Foundation's ministry on campus: "Wesley Foundation is the traditional name for Methodist religious activities on a state university or private college campus. As an educational institution of the Methodist Church, it attempts ministering to the total religious life of the church in the university community. Its objectives are to lead students to become followers of Jesus Christ and to help them find a vital personal relationship with God; to develop a supporting group in which individuals will strengthen one another in Christian living through worship, wholesome recreation, study and discussion, social action and stewardship; and to help create a new world order (the Kingdom of God) embodying Christian ideals....." His definition contains a significant clue to understanding the rapid changes then taking place in the focus of a collegiate effort on campus, that of ministering to the total life of the university community. While the efforts of Wesley Foundations were to remain primarily focused on students, the changing emphasis was on a ministry to the university community as a whole, including faculty and staff, and on the presence of the church. In short, the work was no longer exclusively student work but campus ministry in a wider frame.

The article continued, "The Wesley Foundation is the means by which the church follows its students in their transformation from Christian youth to adult churchmen. It is not apart from the church: it is the church at work in the university. Students are trained in churchmanship, and all that is done is in the framework of the church as it makes the necessary adaptation to the university community. True effectiveness of the program must be judged in terms of its expression in post-college life." His call

THE SHINING OF LIGHT: A HISTORY OF THE WESLEY FOUNDATION AT THE UNIVERSITY OF TENNESSEE, 1922-2007

for a recognition of students as *young adults* rather than *youth* was being heard around the country.

In the first several years of the 1950s, the UTK campus was expanding to accommodate a larger student body and a more diverse curriculum, with a major geographical campus shift westward into an area largely occupied by the long-established residences. In 1951, plans were announced for the building of a large university activities center at the corner of Cumberland Avenue and 16th Street, to be named the Carolyn P. Brown University Center. (Since the 1942 fire, there had been no major University building designed for student activities as had been provided by the "Y" Building.) Many Wesley Foundation students (and others) hoped that the plans for the new activities center would include an interdenominational prayer chapel in the heart of the busy campus. When it became apparent that no such chapel was to be included, the Wesley Foundation Council decided (under the leadership of 1952-1953 President James B. Nance, and other officers, Elizabeth Walker, Kenneth Smith and Ruth McWilliams) to create a "personal devotions chapel" of their own in the basement of the house at 908 Temple Avenue, to be open and available to the entire campus.

A materials and supplies budget of $1000 for the project was organized, to which students committed to finding pledges, and they announced vigorously that they would do the manual labor themselves. With difficulty, funds were raised, and the work proceeded. A basement storage room was cleared, and in the austere, window-less space new interior walls and a ceiling were installed, and new linoleum block flooring was laid. The chapel's dimensions were determined by the space available: eight feet wide, eight feet high, thirty feet in length. A limed-oak altar and two matching lecterns were ordered from Hiwassee College Crafts. Pews were ordered from the Roswell Seating Company, Roswell, GA. The intimate apse space was lighted by two concealed ceiling

LAST DAYS ON TEMPLE AVENUE
(1951-1956)

spotlights. About the central imagery of the chapel, an undated newspaper clipping (still in the Foundation's files) declared, "...Since there will be nothing to distract, the student's attention will be focused on the altar from the moment he enters the door."

When finished, the chapel had a chancel rail, a central aisle, and two rows of short pews, with a normal seating capacity of twenty people. Resembling the stark simplicity of early European Protestant chapels, the space was used for meditation and prayer, for small Holy Communion services and for special worship experiences for small cell groups. An outside basement-level entrance accessible from Temple Avenue by a special walkway allowed students – any students, of any faith -- to use the chapel at any time from 8 a.m. to 10 p.m. daily. It was the first chapel on the UTK campus.

Meditation Chapel on Temple Avenue

Students appealed directly for funds for the project from local Methodist Churches. Jimmy Nance and Keith McCord, both from Alamo, TN, appeared before the Methodist Men's Club of Fountain City to seek support. (Keith McCord was chairman of the "Extension Committee.") In a newspaper article in spring 1953, it was reported, "...(the chapel) will serve the students through worship services and will be open at all times for private devotions. Committees are hard at work devising means of raising money, and every effort is being made to complete the work by early May. It will be the first chapel on the U.T. campus." The chapel construction was completed in late summer 1953. When the final "Wesley Foundation Chapel Fund" report was made, expenses showed a balance of $4.18 remaining of the funds raised. Among contributors (alumni and "interested individuals") were Ira N. Chiles, W.L. Ambrose, A.R. Murphy, Claude Vance, Faye Hammond, in addition to the "Fountain City Men's Club" and the "Church Street Official Board." Ira Chiles contributed funds for the purchase of four recessed fluorescent light fixtures at a cost of $59.42, which were installed by Glen Martin.

In order to defray expenses for the chapel, Wesley Foundation students raised $203.45 from a "Cake Auction," and sold scrap lumber from the original storage room for $40.00. Personal contributions from students totaled $130.65. Contributing members of the Wesley Foundation Board were Neal D. Peacock, C.P. Hardin, George H. Smith, William C. Walkup, James Wilder, Dan Hamilton, Jr., and Glen O, Martin. A new brass Sudbury cross for the altar was the gift of the Church Street Methodist youth director, Angela Brown, as a tribute to her father, inscribed *"In Honor of Harvey C. Brown, Church Street Methodist Church, 1926-1933."* A bronze outdoor cross was the gift of Norman Edwards; a dossal cloth was given by Charles Barber. The dream had been realized.

2

The 1952-1953 Wesley Foundation brochure listed twelve committees, headed by Bob Bratcher, Ann Hitt, Faye Hammond, Dorothy Dugger, Anne Dillard, Peggy Speck, Sue Nottingham, Elaine Browder, Sally Thornton, Anne Houser, Jewell Piercy, Jo

LAST DAYS ON TEMPLE AVENUE
(1951-1956)

Henry, and Dick Gamble. A Fellowship Evening for Married Students was held on Friday nights at 8:00 p.m. Thursday Evening "Firesides" featured presentations on topics such as "The Church's Outreach in Missions," "True Evangelism on the Campus," "Understanding Ourselves," "Drama in the Church," and a drama by Foundation students. Bible Study, held at a 5:30 p.m. supper meeting in the "U.T. Cafeteria" was defined as "a discussion of how the Bible came to be and what it means....Questions are asked and faced frankly. New interest will be added this year by the publication of a new translation of the Old Testament. " Featured events of the year included a Fall Retreat, a Winter Banquet, and a Spring Retreat. "Large groups go by truck to the mountains for relaxation and inspiration. Speakers and small groups discuss the theme of the retreat and outdoor worship services are held. Ballgames, swimming, hiking and other sports make for a full week-end, so that no one notices how hard the beds are..." Methodist Churches listing the times of their Sunday services in the brochure included Central, Church Street, Epworth, First, Fountain City, Magnolia Avenue, and Park City.

On Retreat, early 1950s

THE SHINING OF LIGHT: A HISTORY OF THE WESLEY FOUNDATION AT THE UNIVERSITY OF TENNESSEE, 1922-2007

An additional format in which Wesley Foundation's ministry was promoted in 1952-1953 was by means of a pink desk blotter with a listing of activities. Another flyer discussed financial support: "Two-thirds of the total current budget of the Wesley Foundation is provided by the church-at-large through Annual Conference and national World Service appropriations. The balance must be raised each year in contributions from local churches, students, alumni, and interested individuals. The average cost per Methodist student in the University is six dollars per year. Some individuals and organizations like to contribute to the current budget in multiples of that amount, feeling thereby that they are paying the way of one or more students....."

Glen Martin was soon honored by the National Student Workers' Association (a forerunner of the National Campus Ministry Association) with his election as its president. At this time, the Wesley Foundation at UTK was regarded nationally as an exemplary organization. At a national meeting at Scarritt College, Nashville, a second honor for Glen Martin came with the adoption of a report on "The Philosophy of Student Work for Wesley Foundations and Other Church-Related Groups," prepared under his chairmanship. Characteristic of Glen's skills was the ability to develop local programming and also to participate fully in state, regional and national activities, particularly those of the Methodist Student Movement, such as the quadrennial conference at the University of Kansas in Lawrence, December 1953-January 1954, to which he accompanied a delegation from the UTK Wesley Foundation. A highlight of this conference, long remembered, was a major address by Dr. Harold Bosley (pastor of First Methodist Church, Evanston, Illinois), who urged the thousands gathered to become involved in the tasks and the journey of social change. His suggestion was to "...pack your bags, get your friends and *hurry* – we've just got time to make it!"

LAST DAYS ON TEMPLE AVENUE
(1951-1956)

In 1953-1954, the new meditation chapel was being utilized for Early Holy Communion every Friday morning. A featured speaker during the year was Dr. Andrew D. Holt, then an administrative assistant to University President C.E. Brehm. Mac Mauney served as president of the Wesley Foundation Council; other elected officers were Marian Wilson, Laurice Holloway and Quentin Alexander. There was an active cadre of other student leaders, including Betty Thompson, Hazel Layman, Kay Arrants, Charles Short, Bob Bratcher, John Wilford and Dick Gamble.

Playing hobo on Temple Avenue

By 1954, a study committee of the Church's Department of College and University Religious Life had issued a position paper entitled, "Standards for Wesley Foundation," listing guidelines for organization, personnel, facilities, and finances. In the area of program, there was a major emphasis on 'training for churchmanship," whereby students were given the means "to know the Church program as the body of Christ, as the custodian of values, as the universal fellowship of believers, and as the agency of ideals, functioning in community to build a new social order." The position paper affirmed the philosophy of the Methodist Student Movement as part of the University Christian Movement, declaring boldly that ".....The Campus Christian Movement.....is the church, the church at work in the university experience. Students are to be trained in

35

THE SHINING OF LIGHT: A HISTORY OF THE WESLEY FOUNDATION AT THE UNIVERSITY OF TENNESSEE, 1922-2007

churchmanship.....The greatest experience of Christendom in our day is the ecumenical movement. This means awakening, witnessing, evangelizing and uniting....As Methodists we can be no less than what we are as we work with others....'That all may be one.'" The thrill and challenge of the ecumenical movement was in the air. The UTK Wesley Foundation was awarded a "Certificate of Accreditation" in 1954, having met the necessary standards. Significantly, among the signers of the certificate was Harvey C. Brown, then secretary of the Department. Four years later, in 1958, the Certificate of Accreditation was renewed, and again was signed by Harvey C. Brown.

Beginning in the 1920s, a significant by-product of the *community* of the Wesley Foundation was the establishment of a network of friendships which lasted – and still lasts. Such a network of close friends in the mid-1950s included Lucinda Alsobrook-Burbach, Agnes Beard Adair, Martha Corry Alexander, Benjamin and Mary Nell Rogers, Judy Meneely, and David and Roberta Bagwell.

Second Methodist Church was the scene of the April 12, 1957 Spring Banquet, its theme "World Brotherhood," advertised as an "international type banquet." The theme was developed by Peggy Lee Jones and Judy Meneely. The theme of the 1957 Spring Retreat (on May 11-12) was "Not I, But Christ," planned by Charles Arnold and Shirley Delapp. The Wesley Foundation Choir elected its officers -- Harold Childress, president; Jack Phillips, vice-president; and Peggy Raulston, secretary-treasurer.

A publication of the Wesley Foundation during the 1950s was *motive at u.t.,*" published monthly. In an issue dated February 1956, plans for a "Christian Witness Mission" were discussed, as part of the Knoxville District Mission held January 27-February 3. There were announcements of a Drama Club, then in rehearsal for *This Night Shall Pass*. The annual Wesley Foundation banquet was

LAST DAYS ON TEMPLE AVENUE
(1951-1956)

to be held at Church Street Church on March 24. The editor in 1956 was Peggy House, and writers included Henry Evans, Lucinda Alsobrook, and Quentin Alexander. Wesley Foundation alumni mentioned in this issue mentioned were Mary Lou Sawyer Cathey, Dick and Elaine Browder Davidson, Vance and Marian Wilson Eastridge, Ruth Ellen Kelley Riley, and Charles and Kay Arrants Short.

Significantly, the February 1956 issue was one of the last issues of *motive at u.t.* to bear the familiar picture of the house at 908 Temple Avenue. The University was actively seeking property in the heart of the campus on which to expand, and the choice corner lot occupied by the Wesley Foundation was a prime target, identified as the proposed location for the new Claxton Education Building. As early as November 1954, Glen Martin had urgently requested Harley Fowler, President of the Hamilton National Bank in Knoxville and a member of the UTK Board of Trustees, to contact University authorities about their obvious intention to acquire the Wesley Foundation's property. Mr. Fowler wrote to President Brehm, seeking clarification of this process, and asking where the Foundation was to move – "In view of the situation of the Wesley Foundation, I think this is a matter which should be given immediate consideration and disposed of by the Executive Committee in plenty of time so that this institution will not be prejudiced by our suddenly pouncing on them without any place for them to settle down….."

Negotiations continued about a "good nearby situation" to be provided in exchange for the Temple Avenue property, and by early 1956 an arrangement between the University and the Foundation had finally been concluded.

Days in the Sprankle house were numbered. Alumni still remember their concern about losing the prime location, the familiar surroundings of the Center building and the new basement meditation chapel on which they had worked diligently. Angst about the future clouded the end of the 1955-1955 academic year.

Entrance to the Meditation Chapel

Chapter IV

MELROSE PLACE
(1956-1960)

1

With the assistance of Dr. Andrew D. Holt, a supporter of the Wesley Foundation and an active member of Church Street Methodist Church, a "good nearby situation" into which the campus ministry could move was indeed secured. A legal assignment executed on February 8, 1956 named members of the Wesley Foundation Board as "assignors" -- Herbert L. Lee, E.E. Lundy, Ira N. Chiles, J.W. Hoffman, H.G. Loy, Ralph W. Mohney, George H. Smith, Paul E. Brown and Marvin S. Kincheloe, who were identified as "trustees for the Methodist Student Center." The Wesley Foundation was named as "assignee." Involved was a "Contract for Exchange of Properties," in which the Wesley Foundation agreed to convey 908 Temple Avenue to the University, for which they were to be paid $10,000 in cash, in exchange for university-owned property at "1718 Melrose Avenue."

Also contained in the assignment was permission for the Foundation to remove the heating plant from the Temple house, as well as the new fixtures from the basement chapel, and to convey the "said respective properties" by a warranty deed. The assignors entered into the contract which was then adopted at a meeting of the Holston Annual Conference in Chattanooga on June 9, 1956. The necessary warranty deed was finally executed, legally conveying the Temple Avenue property to the University "for and in consideration of the sum of One Dollar ($1.00)."

THE SHINING OF LIGHT: A HISTORY OF THE WESLEY FOUNDATION AT THE UNIVERSITY OF TENNESSEE, 1922-2007

In anticipation of the move, the Board of Directors (on July 19, 1956) formed a Charter of Incorporation, naming the institution officially and legally as "The Wesley Foundation at the University of Tennessee, Inc." The document was signed by Cecil P. Hardin, Neal D. Peacock, Robert H. Duncan, S.H. Everett, George H. Smith, Glenn E. Smith, Marvin S. Kincheloe, Herbert L. Lee, Gladstone I. Teasley, D. Trigg James, and Glen Otis Martin. Its stated purpose was "…to provide for the religious, intellectual and social care of persons related to the University of Tennessee in Knoxville, especially those who are adherents of The Methodist Church….."

There was uncertainty among both the student leadership and members of the Board of Directors that the move from Temple Avenue would remove the locus of ministry too far from the heart of the campus, for Melrose Place seemed to be (in student terms) "out on the edge of nowhere." (Actually, it was only approximately two blocks away). In earlier years, Melrose Place and Melrose Avenue (in a prestigious development once called Melrose Park) had been known popularly as "Millionaires' Row," for it had housed some of Knoxville's wealthiest citizens, notably the Ashe, Frantz, McNutt, Tyson, Van Deventer, Staub, Briscoe, McDowell, Kuhlman and Vestal families. The house on Melrose Place was a large Queen Anne stone and shingle residence designed by architects Barber & Klutz, and built by contractor James R. McDowell in 1906-1907. By 1924, the house had been sold to the family of druggist Nathan B. Kuhlman; as late as 1964, neighbors along Melrose Place remembered that Mrs. Pearl Kuhlman maintained the "most beautiful azalea garden in Knoxville" on the upper part of the property. The family of Charles L. Rader, Jr. bought the house by 1934. Then, briefly, the J.L. Neely, Jr. family owned the house, after which it was acquired by the University. It was rented by the Episcopal Church for the use of the Tyson House Episcopal Center, and then for two years (1952-1954) it was rented by a UTK fraternity.

MELROSE PLACE
(1956-1960)

Next door, at the corner of Melrose Place and Lake Avenue, was the home of the E.M Vestal family. Directly across the street from the Foundation was the ornate Briscoe house, built in 1897. (In 1964, neighbors recalled that every room in the Briscoe house was paneled in a different wood, and that J.E. and Isabella Briscoe had arranged to have it built during their year-long honeymoon in Europe.) Behind the property, on Terrace Avenue, lived John Fouche Brownlow and his wife Margaret Clark Brownlow, in a house they had built in 1922, after the original Brownlow mansion on Main Street was demolished. (Margaret Brownlow, who lived into her late nineties, became a good friend of the Wesley Foundation.) Not far away, where Melrose Hall, the men's residence hall built in 1946 was located, entrenchments dug by the forces of Union general Ambrose Burnside had been extended in November 1863, anticipating the Battle of Fort Sanders.

The crowning achievement on the hill above the McDowell-Kuhlman house was a large, Italianate villa at 1702 Melrose Avenue, with an imposing central tower, which could be seen at a great distance perched on the promontory. It was one of Knoxville's grandest residences, and had been the scene of elaborate, legendary entertaining. Among its interior features was a graceful, curving staircase in the central hallway and a ceiling probably hand-painted by an artist named Haupt. Built by John J. Craig ca 1858, and originally named Lucknow, it had survived the Battle of Fort Sanders intact. In the early 1870s, the house was sold to Judge Oliver Perry Temple, a jurist, author and a trustee of the University, whose wife, Scotia Caledonia Hume Temple, renamed it Melrose. (Popularly, it was known as "Melrose Hall.") Later owners were Thomas J. Powell and Knoxville mayor John Thomas O'Connor, whose widow Fannie O'Connor continued to live there until 1924. Subsequently, it was converted to the Melrose Art Center and the Melrose Apartments. Melrose was demolished in the late 1950s, to make way for the building of a new high-rise residence hall (later named Hess Hall) on the same site.

According to J. Preston Hess, the circular course of Melrose Place followed the original curving drive by which carriages and later automobiles had accessed the Craig-Temple house from Cumberland Avenue, for the entire expanse of territory now occupied between Hess Hall and Cumberland Avenue was the ornamental, Italian-style lawn planned by the Temples in the 1870s. An ornamental lake was dug at the bottom of the property, thus giving present-day Lake Avenue its name.

In 1956, the "new" Wesley Foundation house (then still called the "McDowell house" or the "Kuhlman house" by older neighbors) had vestiges of the imposing structure it once had been, but there was significant structural deterioration, and repairs were needed. Topped by a green Italian tile roof, the Bedford stone and cypress shingle house featured a spacious vestibule, a living room, a dining room, a marble-floored sun room, a butler's pantry and a kitchen on the first floor. An imposing walnut staircase rose from the vestibule to the second floor, where there were four bedrooms and two bathrooms. On the third floor were two large spaces with built-in bookcases fronted by leaded-glass doors. A separate servants' staircase led from the kitchen to the second floor, and a narrow staircase rose from the second to the third floor. There was also a full basement, including a coal room. In the rear of the property was a carriage house-garage with rooms above it, originally used as servants' quarters. The back yard contained massive oak, tulip poplar and magnolia trees planted probably at the time of the house's construction.

Soon, concerns about the new location as being "off the beaten track" and "out of the way" were allayed, for the university was rapidly moving west, directly into the Melrose area. (When vast tracts of faculty residences on Rose Avenue were demolished

MELROSE PLACE
(1956-1960)

The Old Wesley Foundation House

to make room for the Presidential complex of high-rise residence halls, students termed the area "Hiroshima West.") And other church centers on the string of private properties immediately adjacent to University land were being planned. Within a few years, the new Tyson House Episcopal Center was built on the northeastern corner of Melrose Place and Lake Avenue, followed in 1962 (next door to the Wesley Foundation) by the Catholic Student Center, housed initially in the Edward J. Ashe residence. Around the corner from the Catholic Center, the Baptist Student Center (on Melrose Avenue) was situated, occupying the English vernacular-style Calvin Holmes house built in 1922. Later, the Presbyterian Student Center and the Christian Student Center were developed on Melrose Avenue. The neighboring of campus religious institutions caused many students to term Melrose Place and Melrose Avenue "Holy Ghost Row."

When the Wesley Foundation changed its location to Melrose Place in 1956, the campus ministry entered into a new phase of its life. Once again, as in 1943, painting and refurbishing took place in preparation for the 1956-1957 academic year. A wall had previously been removed between the living and dining rooms, and this open space on the main floor became the combination student lounge and dining room, the site of Thursday evening Firesides. There remained impressive touches from the original 1906-1907 construction – set in the bricks above the living room fireplace was a cream-colored plaster copy of a marble frieze depicting the "Cantoria" (the Singing Gallery) by Renaissance sculptor Luca Della Robbia (1400-1482), said to illustrate Psalm 150, "Praise the Lord." (The original of "Cantoria" remains in the Museo dell'Opera del Duomo in Florence, Italy, and shows an extensive panel of ten consecutive panels. The McDowell house frieze depicted only three of the original panels, "Voices," "Horns" and "Drums.") This frieze was later transferred to the new building in 1967, and placed permanently in the library wall. In the west wall of the original dining room of the McDowell house was a

MELROSE PLACE
(1956-1960)

horizontal, mullioned window with prismed edges which reflected the afternoon sun.

Offices, a living room and a library-study room were organized on the second floor. On the third floor, spaces for male students had previously been created when the house was occupied by the fraternity. A third-floor cedar-lined walk-in closet had been converted to a bathroom. From 1956 to 1966 there was concern that in case of fire an exit from this upper space might be difficult if not impossible. Students rigged a rope ladder by which they could lower themselves onto the stone terrace below. The heat of summertime created sweltering living conditions on the third floor. Other living spaces for UTK students were arranged in the basement around the coal furnace and in the rooms above the garage. Students renting spaces in the Wesley Foundation had kitchen privileges, and the out-dated, main floor kitchen was in constant use.

2

During the next academic year (1956-1957), the desirability of the new location, the costly repairs on the 50-year-old McDowell house and the long-range needs of the institution prompted lengthy discussions in meetings of the Board of Directors concerning the future. As a result, planning was begun for a new structure on the same site – a modern Wesley Foundation building designed according to the needs of a functioning collegiate ministry. Financial resources were limited, and there was an initial recognition that the new structure would have to be built in stages, but clearly the time had come for a physical plant that would declare a clear statement of both Methodist presence and the vitality of campus ministry.

The Board commissioned a set of plans by the eminent architect Charles Barber, of the firm of Barber & McMurry, for a building which would accommodate the long, sharply sloping lot fronting Melrose Place. Within a few months, architectural plans presented to the Board, estimated to cost approximately $190,000, were a sharp contrast to the aging Queen Anne dwelling. The architect's drawing of the proposed structure appeared in *The Knoxville News-Sentinel.* It showed a Chapel on the upper level, with a tall, square tower bearing a large cross. Adjacent to the chapel was a building featuring horizontal banks of windows under flat roofs at several levels, not unlike public school construction of the time. There were to be classrooms, a staff apartment and residential spaces for students. The newspaper caption read: "Proposed Wesley Foundation -- Methodist students at U-T will find practicality and 'spiritual beauty' in this plan for a new center....." The entire plan was submitted to the Holston Conference, and was approved. It was widely agreed that Conference acceptance of the project reflected not only a desire to provide for the needs of the campus ministry, but was a positive tribute to the work done by J. Irvin McDonough and Glen Otis Martin and their successive student communities.

The first unit of the "master plan" (the Chapel unit) was to be built on the upper level of the lot where Mrs. Kuhlman's azalea garden had been located. (The original, boxy shape of the Chapel first proposed was later significantly changed.) Until the remainder of the building could be built, it was planned that the Wesley Foundation would continue to operate in both the house and the detached chapel, separated by the original driveway. (Mystery exists about the whereabouts of the Wesley Foundation's original set of Charles Barber's complete "master plan" drawings. For several years after the completion of the Chapel, the drawings were kept in the Foundation's files, but they then disappeared -- borrowed perhaps and never returned, or accidentally destroyed.) Largely because of successive financial considerations, the additional phases of the first master plan were never built as

MELROSE PLACE
(1956-1960)

originally designed. The completion of the building dream would not come to fruition for more than ten years.

During the Thanksgiving season 1957, ground was broken for the new Chapel; the gold-plated spade belonging to Church Street Methodist Church was used. George H. Smith, one of the longtime advocates of the Wesley Foundation and president of the newly incorporated Board, turned the first spade of earth. Gathered for the historic moment, captured in a surviving photograph, were J. Preston Hess, Robert H. Duncan, the architect Charles Barber, George H. Smith, Glen Otis Martin and Herbert L. Lee. Sam Sims, president of the Student Council for 1957-1958, was there, as were other student leaders Martha Corey, Betty Patterson, and Lynn Testerman.

The Chapel featured a solid brick façade, thrusting the construction upward and anchoring the entire property. The interior red brick apse contained a series of inset brick crosses and a set of three mosaic-covered niches. A wrought-iron cross was suspended from the ceiling over the altar, *in medias res*. The remarkable wooden ceiling and beams were hand-painted by Hugh C. Tyler, a well-known ecclesiastical artist, who "lay on his back like Michelangelo" (as neighbors said) to reach all the upper space. Mr. Tyler, the uncle of novelist James Agee, had lived as a child and young man in the Fort Sanders neighborhood, but by 1957 was a resident of Connecticut. He returned to Knoxville often to execute church designs. Among other interior Knoxville church decorations he completed are to be found today at Church Street United Methodist Church, St. John's Episcopal Church, and Second Presbyterian Church.

The colorful Chapel ceiling designs, reminiscent of medieval Flemish ceilings, featured a blue background emblazoned with stars, and showed shields (topped alternately by chalices and

THE SHINING OF LIGHT: A HISTORY OF THE WESLEY FOUNDATION AT THE UNIVERSITY OF TENNESSEE, 1922-2007

steeples) containing most of the traditional symbols of the Western Church. The exposed wooden beams contained a variety of designs, including the Native American symbol of peace. (The originally bright hues have mellowed to soft, still arresting colors.) Some of the short pews purchased for the meditation chapel at 908 Temple Avenue were utilized, as was the oak altar and the two oak lecterns. An electric organ was soon purchased as the chapel instrument. The brass cross given in memory of Harvey C. Brown was placed on the altar.

The glass windows at the rear of the Chapel were originally to have been fashioned in rich stained glass to depict "The Wesleys," (John, Charles, Samuel and Susannah) as designed by the Willett Company of Philadelphia. (The original colored designs are still extant.) But the expensive stained glass windows were never installed because the Foundation's Chapel finances were depleted before the project was completed, and funds were not available. In place of the stained glass window, plain clear glass filled the space. The total cost of the Chapel was $28,000. By the time of its completion, it still lacked the proposed light fixtures said to match the wrought-iron ceiling supports. A lighting firm in Knoxville donated temporary aluminum fixtures which still remain.

Immediately the Chapel became a much-used place for worship (Morning Devotions and Vespers), for weddings, for Holy Communion -- and for personal *quiet*. It was used not only by active Wesley Foundation students but by other students who sought it as a place for private prayer and reflection. It was easily accessible because it could be entered through its own exterior door. The Chapel was often termed "...the only *really quiet* place on campus." Throughout the years, when votive candles were placed in the brick inserts in the apse and lighted (especially during the Advent season), the entire brick wall appeared to be transfigured by an interior incandescence. There, the shining of light offered memories for generations of students.

3

Wesley Foundation Council officers for 1957-1958 were president Fran Traugott, vice-president Betty Patterson, secretary Peggy Raulston, and treasurer Luther Wilhelm. Other Council leaders were Eddie Sterling (Christian Outreach); Sheila Young (World Christian Community); Lynn Testerman (*motive at u-t);* Larry Hewgley (Publicity); Jack Huffman (Circulation Manager); Jack Phillips (National Motive and Librarian); and Barbara Norman (Food).

The later years of the decade of the 1950s experienced a vigorous, growing ministry of the Wesley Foundation with major involvement in state and regional activities – and particularly with the national Methodist Student Movement. There were outreach programs at Pittman Center and Wesley House Community Center, and there were active deputation-interpretation teams at work in the three supporting Districts (Knoxville, Maryville, Morristown). Within these latter years of the so-called "Silent Generation" on the UTK campus, there was a growing awareness among many in the Wesley Foundation community that perceptions of the meaning of the church were changing.

By 1958, the staff had been expanded to include Charles Arnold as Director of Drama; among the productions of that year was the play *January Thaw,* which raised funds for an ambitious student project -- to purchase a new Volkswagen Microbus to replace an earlier vehicle (a Chevrolet station wagon) acquired in 1951. (In the files there is correspondence about a possible transaction in which a new bus might be obtained with the assistance of a Foundation alumnus, Dick Collins, then living in Troyes, France.) Fred and Shirley Delap served as Counselors to

Married Students. (Charles Arnold and the Delaps each received a compensation of $50 per month.) George H. Smith, the distinguished layman sometimes called "Mr. Methodist," continued to serve as President of the Board until his retirement in March 1963.

Left to right:
**Fred Delap,
Shirley Delap,
Glen O. Martin**

In 1958-1959 the total Wesley Foundation budget was $16,880; the combined salary and housing allowance of the director was $6800. The rental of rooms in the Melrose house raised a yearly amount of $1700. A new building fund had been established to seek funds for the completion of the building project, and $1900 was raised. Students serving on the Program Committee of the Board in 1958-1959 were Sudie Doughton, Martha Corry, John Sims and Luther Wilhelm. An large delegation of 28 delegates from the UTK Foundation attended the Sixth Quadrennial Methodist Student Movement Conference in Topeka, Kansas from December 27, 1957 – January 1, 1958; delegates were sent to a Regional Leadership Training Conference at Lake Junaluska, June 9-16, 1958.

Of great significance in September 1958 was the offer of Mrs. Zach T. Godwin, who had recently retired as a residence hall

MELROSE PLACE
(1956-1960)

housemother, to live in the Wesley Foundation building for the purpose of acting as hostess and chaperone, as well as "answering the telephone at times and doing such other light tasks as would be convenient and within her sphere of knowledge and experience." In return, she expected only a room and "perhaps some kitchen privileges." The Board readily accepted her offer. She occupied the large back bedroom on the second floor, and immediately became a gracious, friendly, motherly presence. Myrtle Godwin, sometimes known as "Mother Godwin," was an integral part of the Foundation's life, and was beloved by many students. In later years, when alumni reflected on their experience in the campus ministry, it was often Mrs. Godwin whom they remembered most of all.

Jack Looney served as student president in 1958-1959; Lynn Testerman was vice-president, and Carolyn Thomas was secretary. Minutes of Council meetings show an expanding program. Sudie Doughton headed a new committee, "The Concerned," which emphasized "the world situation." The theme of the annual banquet was "We Gather Together," organized by banquet chairperson Mary Kate Keeble, with Lynn Robinson and Ann Bletner, assistants. Monies raised for the new Volkswagen

On Retreat, late 1950s

THE SHINING OF LIGHT: A HISTORY OF THE WESLEY FOUNDATION
AT THE UNIVERSITY OF TENNESSEE, 1922-2007

Microbus totaled $1235; at work on raising funds were David Davis, Cliff Goodlett, Milton Diehl and Carolyn Moncrief. The Spring Retreat featured "messages by Dr. Ray Short, slides from the Holy Land, a Galilean service at the lake, and discussion groups." By May 1959, a fall retreat was already being organized, led by Eugenia DeFriese, Wayne Harr, Mary Conner and Nancy Squires.

The 1959-1960 Council experienced vigorous student leadership, led by president Margie Millard, vice-president Dwight Wade, secretary Judy Hardy, and treasurer Cliff Goodlett. This year probably represents one of the high points in the skillfulness and resolve of the student leadership to plan, coordinate and implement the year's program. Other students chairing committees were John Goodell (Worship), James Clemmer (Music), David Davis (Publicity), Virginia Klepser (Deputations), David Davis (Publicity), and Juanita Bass (*motive at u.t.*). In addition to the usual welcoming brochure, a special program flyer was produced, featuring a picture of the interior of the Wesley Foundation Chapel, and stating as a "Reason For Being," that the Foundation "...is not a substitute for the worshipping congregation of the local church. Every student is urged to find a Methodist Church home in Knoxville....Yet it is in a significance sense The Methodist Church at work upon the campus. It seeks to minister to the religious, intellectual and social needs of those who are members of the campus community." At Bible Study on Tuesdays, the book *The Gospel According to Mark* by Edmund Perry was studied. There were Thursday night Fireside Chats. There were special programs for married students, and a new Methodist Faculty Fellowship had been organized, meeting on the third Thursday of each month. The Foundation was a member of the Beta Iota chapter of the National Society of Wesley Players.

The academic year 1959-1960 was increasingly busy – and momentous. A total of twelve UTK male students lived on the

MELROSE PLACE
(1956-1960)

premises. The drama, Sutton Vane's *Outward Bound,* was produced. On Saturdays, students parked cars for UTK football games on the "Wesley grounds" for $1.00 per car. The money raised was allocated in support of the work of Sam Sims, formerly a student president, and a three-year-missionary in the Philippines. Students leading Chapel services (at 7:30 a.m. and 10:00 p.m.) included Irene Woodward, Dick Peugeot, Carolyn Thomas, Janice Rowland, Eugenia DeFriece, June Hencely, and Jean Turner. Weekly schedules appearing in *motive at u.t.* showed activities every day and every evening of the week. Glen Martin expressed to the Board of Directors his concern that the reduced Annual Conference appropriation to the Wesley Foundation of $11,000 for the year 1960-1961 was inadequate for the breadth of ministry needed; accordingly, he suggested that the appropriation should be $22,786.

In the late 1950s, UTK male students who occupied the third floor space in the Wesley Foundation included James Clemmer, John Goodell, Ken Hanawalt, Ali Shariatmadari, and Dick Trinko.

In addition to his already heavy schedule, Glen Otis Martin had assumed the directorship of the Tennessee Methodist Student Movement, for which he received no additional compensation; his national stature as a campus minister was rising. It was not surprising to many of his colleagues and to the Wesley Foundation students that in May 1960 he accepted a position on the staff of the Department of College and University Religious Life of the Methodist Board of Education in Nashville, having completed nine eventful and progressive years at UTK. In particular, he had helped issue UTK students more firmly into the wider world of the Methodist Student Movement and the growing movement of ecumenism, while strengthening the local ministry. He had sounded a clear call to discipleship.

THE SHINING OF LIGHT: A HISTORY OF THE WESLEY FOUNDATION
AT THE UNIVERSITY OF TENNESSEE, 1922-2007

Chapel Ground Breaking, 1957, *left to right*, **J.P. Hess, R.H. Duncan, Charles Barber, George Smith, Martha Corey, Betty Patterson, Glen O. Martin, Lynn Testerman, Herbert L. Lee, and Sam Sims**

Chapter V

THE WINDS OF CHANGE
(1960-1964)

1

A new campus minister, George S. Paris, was hired by the Wesley Foundation Board of Directors in April 1960. Well-known in national Wesley Foundation and MSM circles as a man of artistic ability as well as theological acumen, George had recently graduated from Union Theological Seminary in New York, and was already experienced in both the local church as pastor and in "Wesley Foundation work." During the early summer of 1960, the Board of Directors approved the purchase of a parsonage for the Wesley Foundation campus minister. (For several years, Mr. Mack and his family, and then Glen and Jeanne Martin had lived on the second floor of the 908 Temple Avenue house; after the move to 1718 Melrose Place, Glen and Jeanne Martin had lived in a rented apartment nearby.) A property at 4522 Alta Vista Way in Knoxville's Sequoyah Hills was acquired at a cost of $19,500, less a donation of $500 made by the owner. The 1954 frame house contained a living room-dining room, four bedrooms, a kitchen and two bathrooms. A down payment of $3500 was made, and a mortgage of $15,500 was assumed. George and Velma Paris and their four children arrived in Knoxville in July 1960.

George Paris found a well-organized community of student leadership ready for the 1960-1961 academic year, including president James Clemmer, vice-president John Goodell, secretary Virginia Klepser, and treasurer Dwight Wade. Other students who held Council positions were Maggie Kelso, Terry Trimble, Carolyn

Moncrief, Betty McNabb, Clifton Goodlett, Janice Beard, and Nancy Squires – and "team captains" Charline Reeves, Dick Trinko, John Reeves, Gerald Humphreys and Glenda Millard. Juanita Bass, a student who had served as Glen Martin's secretary in the late 1950s and who continued in this role for George Paris, was a vital asset to the Foundation. After her graduation from UTK, she attended Vanderbilt Divinity School, and later received a doctorate from Drew Theological School, Madison, New Jersey, and served for many years with the United Methodist Board of Global Missions in New York City.

Left to right:
**George S. Paris,
Myrtle Godwin,
and James Clemmer**

A feature of the Wesley Foundation's 1960-1961 academic year was significant participation in the University Convocation (in which the "Methodist speaker" was Dr. Ray Allen, head of campus ministry at Lambuth College in Jackson, TN), as well as Fall Retreat and continuing deputation teams. A modern morality play, directed by George Paris, *Let Man Live,* by Par Lagervist was presented in November, featuring players Martha Corry, James Clemmer, Gerald Humphreys, Charline Reeves and Dick Trinko. The role of a "Negro boy lynched for a crime he did not commit," was played by Stanley Wester, a pre-ministerial student from Knoxville College.

THE WINDS OF CHANGE
(1960-1964)

The early 1960s engagement with social issues was expressed by the Council's approval of a proposal by the Presbyterian campus group in support of "undergraduate integration" which was to be read at the UTK Trustees meeting. (The "undergraduate integration" issue was significant because the Supreme Court decision *Brown v Board of Education* had already been in effect for four years, whereby many campuses and Wesley Foundations were already fully desegregated.) A student delegation was sent to the Model United Nations Assembly in Nashville, and a delegate represented the Foundation at a weekend study retreat at the Highlander Folk School in Monteagle, TN, where an opportunity for interracial dialogue was present.

On February 24, 1961, in the highly charged national atmosphere of anti-Communist sentiment, George Paris and John (Jack) Payne, director of the Presbyterian Student Center, distributed mimeographed leaflets entitled "In Search of Truth" outside the campus building where the University R.O.T.C. was showing *Operation Abolition,* a film produced by the House Un-American Activities Committee. The leaflets indicated the serious inaccuracies contained in the film, which purported to show that Communist-inspired agitators had led riots on the West Coast while the Committee was holding public hearings. (Some of the inaccuracies were later acknowledged by the HUAA Committee.) The aim of the two campus ministers was not to prevent the showing of the film but to protest the distortions of truth contained in it. Three days later, on February 27, *The Knoxville Journal,* a conservative newspaper, published an article about the event, and quoted George as saying, "This is really serious if we have to distort the truth to protect Americans. This is one of the points we make to Europeans behind the Iron Curtain in our Radio-Free Europe broadcasts. We give them the truth, and yet the truth is not shown in the movie."

THE SHINING OF LIGHT: A HISTORY OF THE WESLEY FOUNDATION AT THE UNIVERSITY OF TENNESSEE, 1922-2007

At a called meeting of the Executive Committee of the Board of Directors on February 28, 1961, there was consideration of angry protests which had been received from "certain Methodists in the Knoxville vicinity" against the distribution of the leaflets. During the discussion, George made an oral statement, describing his action as one of conscience. A resolution was adopted by the Committee, recognizing the right of the R.O.T.C. to show such a film to its cadets, as well as the University's right to do so "…..if it considers the film to be truthful…in the interest of impartial education." Also recognized was the right of George Paris to have distributed statements "…..if he considered statements in the film to be untruthful." A meeting of the full Board was arranged, in order to continue discussion of the matter.

The full Board met on March 9, 1961, at which time the situation was reviewed. Again attention was focused on the complaints of "outstanding Methodists who were leading in opposition to the director's action," claiming that George's stand appeared to be pro-Communist. Again, George pointed to the nationwide controversy created by the film and its investigation by the National Council of Churches. He affirmed his appreciation of the freedom granted him by the Board and said that he did not intend to abuse or misuse this freedom. His mimeographed statement was distributed to the Board. There followed a discussion during which both opposition to and defense of the director's action were expressed. Dr. Neal Peacock maintained that "…if we fail to take a stand for the right, for fear of possible opposition, we fail to be Christian in the highest sense of the word." History professor Dr. J. Wesley Hoffmann said, "Had Mr. Paris asked me, under the circumstances, to aid in the distribution, I probably would have acted in the affirmative." Student Dwight Wade commented, "Apathy is our besetting sin on the campus at U.T. The emphasis of the Foundation has been to steer each one to become fully involved in all of life…The effectiveness of the Wesley Foundation would be greatly lessened if we seriously

THE WINDS OF CHANGE
(1960-1964)

criticize Mr. Paris for doing what he felt was right." Dr. A.B. Wing noted that unfortunately "many people" considered George's action to be Communist-inspired, and that such an impression needed to be corrected. After George Paris excused himself from the meeting, the group reformulated the Executive Committee's informal resolution, that "while the Board subscribes...to the historic stand of the Methodist Church that there shall be no censorship on the thinking and actions of its ministry," it was nonetheless concerned about George's activities ".....which had impaired his effectiveness as well as that of the Wesley Foundation." It recognized that George had not been aware that his action would be construed as being in defense of Communism and that he had "great potential" for service at the Wesley Foundation. The campus minister was advised to be more discreet in the future, in order that actions were not harmful to the Wesley Foundation's ministry. There was no unanimous agreement about the resolution, and it was agreed that another called meeting was needed, at which time a vote would be taken.

The Board met again on March 16, by which time more community opposition to George's action had been received. More evidences of the distortions contained in the film were discussed. After more consideration, amendments presented succeeded in changing some of the original resolution wording, but there was still no agreement. A committee was appointed to prepare a final resolution. In addition, there was an adjourned meeting which followed, during which further suggestions were made toward resolving the impasse. At a fifth meeting on March 21, 1961, a resolution, carefully crafted by Thomas F. Chilcote and Edgar A. Eldridge, was finally agreed upon as the official response of the Board. Recognizing the encouragement of free communication of ideas as essential to the discovery of truth, it suggested that George had become "unwittingly involved" in distributing information that he considered pertinent regarding "Operation Abolition," and found him to be "anti-Communist without equivocation." The resolution continued by saying that while the director may have acted in good conscience, he was found not to have exercised wisdom and foresight, and the Board now expected him to "…..weigh his words and actions so as not be charged with imprudence and so not to jeopardize the vital ministry of the Wesley Foundation." He was further urged to consult with the chairman of the Executive Committee "…..in regard to any matter that may imperil his effectiveness, the Wesley Foundation's influence, or the integrity of The Methodist Church."

By this time, the Student Council had also taken its own official action in response to the crisis. On March 1, 1961, its minutes recorded, "The Called Meeting was called to order by the president, Jimmy Clemmer. This meeting was held for a clarification of the recent film on campus put out by the House Un-American Activities Committee. Mr. Paris said that they did not protest the film, but that they were opposed to the distortion of truth in it. Mr. Paris and Jack Payne of the Presbyterian Center were tagged Communist since they passed out literature against an anti-Communist film. The Council commended Rev. Paris' stand." Present were James Clemmer, John Goodell, Dwight Wade, Virginia Klepser, Juanita Bass, Janice Beard, Dick Trinko, Lynn Jackson, Glenda Millard, Bo Thomas, Maggie Kelso, Gerald Humphreys, and Charline Reeves.

On March 23, 1961, two days after the last of the series of contentious Board meetings, George Paris issued his annual report. Prior to commenting on student activities, special events, and staff, he stated, "The concern of the Church that the proclamation of God's Word of redemption reach into every aspect of life and culture means that the university campus come forward with this concern….the community of Christians must be alert to trends, thought patterns, cultural developments taking place about them in order that they bring the most effective witness to bear on problems facing the academic community…..The purpose of the

THE WINDS OF CHANGE
(1960-1964)

Wesley Foundation is therefore to enable students and faculty to see and accept their God-given responsibility and to learn how best to carry out this Christian vocation."

An unfortunate current of discontent about George Paris as being "pro-Communist" or "too liberal" or "modernist" in the minds of key laypeople in the three supporting Methodist districts, as well as in the minds of a few Holston Conference officials, became fixed. Such discontent in a conservative theological climate is difficult to change. The storm was to grow stronger.

The Foundation's program continued at a lively pace. A mimeographed weekly publication, *The Methodist Crusader,* appeared for its second year in 1960-1961, offering a day-by-day "Wesley Week at a Wink," with Pat Weir as editor. An art exhibit by Margaret (Peg) Rigg was displayed on the walls of the main room, the sun porch, the entrance hall, the stairway and the upstairs rooms at the Foundation. Other artists displaying works throughout the year were Kermit Ewing, Walter Stevens, Carl Sublett, Robert Birdwell and Richard Clarke. Evening Chapel services were led by Juanita Bass, Clifton Goodlet, Ken Hanawalt, Dwight Wade, Jerry Heimlicker, and Temple Jellicourse. Dr. Ruth Stephens spoke at the Thursday Faculty Luncheon, and Dr. James E. Sellers of Vanderbilt University Divnity School talked with interested students about vocations in theology and religious education.

Working in the Melrose Place kitchen

THE SHINING OF LIGHT: A HISTORY OF THE WESLEY FOUNDATION
AT THE UNIVERSITY OF TENNESSEE, 1922-2007

John Goodell led the 1960-1961 Worship Committee. In a Student Council self-study report, John wrote, "I feel that worship of God should be and is the axle around which the Wesley Wheel turns. In order for our wheel to roll over a true path, it must be guided. This guidance is worked mainly by controlling the axis. This is a poor analogy, but I think that we can see that we must be in constant communion with God as individuals and as a community in order to carry out His will.....Our worship program at Wesley is the main means which we have in maintaining this communion as a community." (John Goodell entered the theological school at Drew University, Madison, N.J., and was awarded an Intern Award in 1964.)

2

Pat Weir (president), Glenda Millard (vice-president), Charline Reeves (secretary) and John Reeves (treasurer) were the elected officers of the 1961-1962 Foundation Council. An assistant director, Edward (Ed) Gibson, a recent graduate of the Boston

Spring Banquet, 1961
Norma Dean Smith, soloist; James Clemmer, pianist

THE WINDS OF CHANGE
(1960-1964)

University School of Theology who had interned at the University of Texas Wesley Foundation, joined the staff at a yearly salary of $4200. Ed had his own quarters in the Wesley Foundation building. In August 1961, George and nine students attended the Seventh Quadrennial Conference of the Methodist Student Movement on the campus of the University of Illinois, its theme "Covenant For a New Creation."

In 1962 and 1963, events on the national stage were focusing increasing attention on American campuses. Escorted by federal marshals, James Meredith registered at the University of Mississippi against a backdrop of intimidation and threats of violence. Throughout the country, protests of students against university authority, against *in loco parentis* regulations, against university control of speaker policies and against the War in Vietnam became commonplace. John Kennedy was assassinated, and Lyndon Johnson assumed the presidency. Martin Luther King led a rally of 200,000 in Washington, D.C.. In Alabama, Governor George Wallace vowed, "Segregation now, segregation tomorrow, segregation forever!" The winds of change were blowing.

Plans for the completion of the Wesley Foundation building project were still under discussion. At a Building Committee meeting on October 8, 1961, the amount of $40,000 for building purposes was reported on deposit from the Holston Conference's Expansion Crusade, and it was projected that by June 1962, the sum would likely be $75,000. It was suggested that by the time the Crusade was finished, an amount of $150,000 would likely have accumulated. With Charles Barber the architect present, it was agreed that the "new building" connecting to the existing chapel could be completed in two stages, the first stage costing approximately $150,000. Mr. Barber was authorized to produce new technical drawings of the first of these stages.

Charline Reeves served as president of the Council in 1962-1963. Other student leaders were Carolyn Varner, Grace Jung, Sabra Dawes, John Williams, James Rugh, Louise Hudson, Charles Reeves, Frankie Ellis, and Albert Wilhelm. The Council was reorganized, comprised of "commissioners" of Evangelism, Finance, Education, Christian Social Concerns, Worship, and The Arts. A special guest speaker in November 1962 was William Swain, on furlough from campus ministry work in Tokyo.

In December 1962, George Paris proposed that the Methodist and Presbyterian Churches develop a "corporate ministry," involving common planning by both staffs and common utilization. The program moved clearly in an ecumenical direction, including Presbyterian student representation on the Wesley Foundation Council. However, separate Foundation events were maintained.

1963 became a pivotal year in Wesley Foundation's history. As an experiment, the Board of Directors approved – upon request of the Student Council -- a service of Morning Worship in the Chapel at 10:30 a.m., not intended to be competitive with local churches but as a way of offering worship to the many students who lived within a couple of blocks of the Wesley Foundation building. The Board's Finance Committee agreed that until an additional $50,000 was available, plans for the construction of a new building should not proceed; authorization was given to borrow $1000 in order to meet current obligations before the close of the Conference year. The worsening structural, plumbing and electrical conditions in the house at 1718 Melrose Place were presenting costly problems.

The Back Door, an innovative Coffee-House experiment located in the renovated basement of the Presbyterian Student Center at 1830 Melrose Avenue, began in February 1963, staffed by Presbyterian campus minister Ewell Reagin and George Paris as

THE WINDS OF CHANGE
(1960-1964)

the core of a supervising committee termed an "informal, unchartered staff." The name derived from the fact that the Coffee House area was entered through the back door of the basement. It was viewed by the staff as a mission, offering a place for conversation, lectures, play readings, poetry readings, music, art exhibits and camaraderie on Friday and Saturday nights from 8:00 p.m. until 12 p.m. Play readings involved the university Speech and Theater Department, which presented excerpts from plays by T.S. Eliot, Jean Paul Sartre, Albert Camus and Edward Albee. Engagement with some of the basic issues of university life was its goal. Both students and faculty as well as occasional community citizens were involved. Among the artists who exhibited work were Margaret (Peg) Rigg, art editor of *motive* magazine, and Joanna Higgs. At its height, in 1963 and early 1964, between 100 and 150 people participated in The Back Door each evening. The Assistant Dean of Liberal Arts was quoted as saying that "…it was the only institution on the campus which was contributing to the real purpose of the University." According to George Paris, the place was "…experimental and not obviously religious in character," and consequently many Knoxville clergy were reluctant to give it their approval.

George contributed his considerable artistic skills to the renovation of The Back Door with great enthusiasm. As a result of this work, he devoted considerable time to his involvement there and increasingly less time to the on-going program of the Wesley Foundation at 1718 Melrose Place. He rightly considered the Coffee House an integral part of the new ecumenical thrust of the Foundation's ministry, but this passion was not universally shared. Criticism of the venture focused on George's absence from his other programmatic work, as well as the avant-garde character of its image. Among some Knoxville District Methodist churches, including Church Street Methodist Church, those already criticial of his methods and his public image found new reasons to complain, labeling the Coffee House as "subversive."

THE SHINING OF LIGHT: A HISTORY OF THE WESLEY FOUNDATION AT THE UNIVERSITY OF TENNESSEE, 1922-2007

In March 1963, George H. Smith, the retired insurance executive and former City Councilman known as "Mr. Methodist," resigned after six terms as president of the Wesley Foundation's incorporated Board, where he had served since 1957. Dr. Neal Peacock, dean of instruction in the UTK College of Agriculture, became the new Board president. George Smith continued to serve as treasurer. An article in *The Knoxville News-Sentinel* noted the Wesley Foundation as "the oldest denominational student group at U-T, organized in the 1920s."

Sunday supper, early 1960s

A sign of the rapidly changing times was a quiet note in Board's Executive Committee minutes (April 5, 1963) that "a young man living at the Wesley Foundation was arrested for disturbing the peace in connection with the integration of a Knoxville eating establishment." Ed Gibson concluded his work as assistant director on May 31, 1963. Mrs. Myrtle Godwin ("Mother Godwin"), the resident hostess who had been a counselor and guide to many UTK students, became ill, and concluded her service in September 1963. Rapid change was the order of the day.

THE WINDS OF CHANGE
(1960-1964)

The Wesley Foundation faced another crisis when *The Knoxville Journal* reported that a sermon entitled "Reluctant Revolution" had been preached by George on August 11, 1963 at the Tennessee Valley Unitarian Church in Knoxville. According to George's report to the Board of Directors, the sermon (which he had prepared in manuscript form) was an honest attempt to discuss "what is happening in Christian theology." (A copy of the sermon, a critique of contemporary theological ideas of the early 1960s, remains in the Foundation's files.) The title of the sermon was derived from a chapter contained in Bishop John A.T. Robinson's book, *Honest to God,* a groundbreaking study of some of the contemporary currents of theology – and, for its time, controversial. In the book a few of the ontological ideas of Paul Tillich, as well as the writings of Rudolf Bultmann and Dietrich Bonhoeffer, were analyzed, concepts by then well established in the world of post-Liberal Protestant thinking.

The sermon began, "No other fact of our common life is clearer to us than the relentless onslaught of radical change." He illustrated the change by discussing developments in the concept of God propounded by Paul Tillich – God as the Ground of Being. "He [God] is not a thing among other things, whose nature and existence can be argued. Rather He is the source and center of all that is. He is not a Being who is present in the good and beautiful but absent from the evil and unlovely. We cannot escape Him in any aspect of life. The Bible bears eloquent testimony to this kind of God and dramatically abhors the God of our own making which can be domesticated and robbed of mystery and power...." The crux of the sermon turned on contrasting this concept of God with the "comfortably established religion of a great many comfortably established churches" where God is "a kind of cosmic bell-hop who comes to our assistance if and when we have need of him." George commented, "By positing a God somewhere 'out there' who responds to our various needs, we have created a situation similar to the one in that era when man believed God to be 'up there' in a three-storied universe." He ended the sermon by challenging his hearers to a new Bonhoeffer-like "worldliness" in which all of life is embraced "with all its duties and problems, its successes and failures, its experiences and helplessness. It is in such a life that we throw ourselves utterly in the arms of God and participate in his sufferings in the world and watch with Christ in Gethsemane."

The front-page *Journal* review of this sermon, on August 12, was entitled "Unitarians Told God Exists in Himself." George, it said, quoted "several 'modernist' theologians that the old concepts of God were not conceived from the Bible but in the minds of theologians who devised them to satisfy the masses." The reviewer discussed his own interpretation of George's words, that "since the middle of the 19th century man has become increasingly aware that God is not 'up there or out there' but in actuality is man himself, and that no God outside of man is necessary." (The reviewer seriously misunderstood or misconstrued the concept of the "Ground of Being.") The newspaper article also analyzed the sermon by concluding that George's point-of-view included the following, "Many free thinkers…are coming to the realization that the old ideas of God should be relegated to the junkpile and that the new image of God through man should be accepted." The reluctant revolution, the reviewer concluded, "revolved around man clinging to the 'old time religion'" as opposed to accepting new thinking.

In a subsequent conversation with the Board, George vigorously affirmed that as a Methodist he was a thoroughgoing Trinitarian; he refuted the newspaper's claim that he "preached" one set of beliefs to a Methodist congregation and another for a "more advanced Unitarians." He explained the many distortions by the *Journal* reporter, and distributed manuscript copies of the sermon.

THE WINDS OF CHANGE
(1960-1964)

The Board of Directors was still beset by the negative reactions in local Methodist churches and in the Knoxville community created by distribution of the "In Search of Truth" leaflets, and the impression (in the minds of some people) that George was pro-Communist. With the publication of the new *Journal* article, criticism became more vociferous. More churches withdrew financial support. More letters of concern were received from clergy and laypeople. The Board met on August 23 to consider the new set of problems. After several hours of discussion, Board members agreed to convene again in an adjourned session on August 30.

In the August 30, 1963 meeting, there was both support for and rejection of George's style of ministry. At issue were his methods and the impact of his actions on the Wesley Foundation ministry, as well as the financial problems the crisis had engendered. After several proposals were considered, amended and debated, it was agreed that he should continue as campus minister through the academic year of 1963-1964, but within the Executive Committee there were clear signs that he would not likely remain after May 1964. Within the Board, George Paris' personal integrity and strength of conscience were not questioned. In his role as pastor-teacher, he had clearly sounded important and prophetic themes: this enlightenment was recognized by students and faculty and others who have long appreciated his ministry.

3

Leadership was offered to the Student Council in 1963-1964 by president Charles Fowler. Albert Wilhelm served as vice-president, Bettye Hall as secretary and William (Perk) Thornton as treasurer. Other student leaders included Andy Petty, James Rugh, James and Charles Reeves, Ann Fox, and Walt Ward. There were drama productions presented by the students in the main room of the Wesley Foundation, including two companion plays by Charles

THE SHINING OF LIGHT: A HISTORY OF THE WESLEY FOUNDATION
AT THE UNIVERSITY OF TENNESSEE, 1922-2007

Williams, *A House By the Stable* and *Grab and Grace,* in addition to *Christ in the Concrete City* by the English playwright P.W. Turner.

During the annual meeting of the Board of Directors on February 28, 1964, it was announced that George Paris had accepted a position as the State Director of the Kansas Methodist Student Movement – and that he would be leaving Knoxville in June. The minutes of the February 28 meeting included Neal Peacock's assessment that ".....the past year has been an interim period of extreme difficulty." The Personnel Committee reported that student president Charles Fowler had been included in their recent meeting, where he "presented the interests of the students in having the successor to the professional director be a person of comparative youthfulness who would understand student life." At the same meeting, it was reported that building problems continued. An outstanding bill of $1093 was approved for payment, involving the purchase of a new boiler for the deteriorating building.

An excellent report from the Student Program Committee was submitted to the Board, outlining work in Missions & Evangelism, Deputations, Tuesday Noon Luncheons, Recreation, Thursday Night Discussions, Sunday Evening Programs, The Back Door Coffee House, Drama and the Student Conference in Athens, Ohio, where a delegation of six students from the UTK Wesley Foundation attended. The student report commented, "...Our work has not been without frustration. We have been concerned over the lack of large attendance. We have tried to vary the emphases of our program in order to interest different groups of students. Another source of frustration is the building in which this meeting is being held. This building is simply not conducive to the operation of a Wesley Foundation in a large university. Although a new building would not insure a greatly expanded program, it would certainly insure a great impetus in that direction....We believe that there are

THE WINDS OF CHANGE
(1960-1964)

certain issues that the Church must face, and that since we are the Church on campus, it is our God-given duty to state our beliefs and to back those beliefs with action....Since this is a large university, it would seem only natural that the new director should be someone who has had training and experience in Wesley Foundation work....."

George Paris' written report to the Board on February 28, 1994 was a passionate, confrontational statement. Noting the rapid secularization on the UTK campus, he described how he had been listening carefully to the views of students about the Church, and reported that "...what the Church has been doing and failing to do has had far more of an impression on college students than 10,000 sermons. In fact, students are struck by a disparity between what is said and what is done and they are deeply distrustful of the church." He challenged the Board to listen to the concerns of students, and commented, "...disruptions and disturbances are inevitable when the Church lives out its mission and you will probably face problems more serious than those concerning myself and *The Knoxville Journal* if you are to do your task as a Board faithfully, but to this I challenge each of you." The report revealed his deep conviction that ".....our denomination is embarrassed by the Methodist Student Movement and wishes to domesticate this unruly stepchild and make it utterly respectable. Students are not asking for a safe and respectable church but a renewed church that is aware and courageous and prepared to be of service to the world."

George Paris left a profound imprint on the Wesley Foundation, still felt today.

4

In spite of the "year of extreme difficulty," talk continued about tearing down the old house at 1718 Melrose Place, and replacing it with a new building, *soon*. Nostalgia for the sixty-year-old structure became more acute, especially among students who had lived there on the third floor and in the basement. Much of the emotion swirled around the gentle presence of the former hostess, Myrtle Godwin. The feelings of sadness were expressed by James Clemmer, a former Student Council president, in a haunting, elegaic poem dated April 5, 1964, entitled "The Old House (For Mrs. Godwin)." Following James' graduation from UTK in 1963, he pursued his studies at Duke University, and became a professor of English at Austin Peay State University in Clarksville, Tennessee.

> I remember our old house best
> in summer, after some departing guest
> wheezes down the staircase in a
> burst of lavender. Some old crone
> to us, but a lifelong friend and
> loved one whose long hair
> and troubled stare never ceased to
> amaze us midnight loiterers,
> after hours,
> when confronted on the rickety stair.
> That was in mimosa time too,
> when the very eves and cellars
> of the old house reeked with a
> sick lovely perfume that confounded
> the squirrels and pigeons and made them
> sick and lovely also.
> It too was beautiful in its day –
> that was your day also –
> and you were beautiful also.
> It is all so mysterious!
> To rack, ruin, sickness and decay
> come all things.
>
> Yet I remember
> our old house in summer at

THE WINDS OF CHANGE
(1960-1964)

nightfall, when the twilight air
hovers so very still in the hedge row,
and the mimosa quivers with the
footsteps of a silent squirrel.
The world then stands ready to forget
the ravages of time, and the ancient
dame at the window ledge stands
within the shadows of the past,
half here and half there,
intrigued again by the loving presence
of a seller of shoes and his children.
Of a bout with influenza and a
train ride so far far away;
taunted also by an unbelieving new
generation of coca cola and hotdog buns,
streaming up and down the stair
searching for new ways to
disturb the possessor of age and time,
of wisdom and decay,
searching for a stereo Savior.

I remember our old house at dawn
after sleepless nights, when the earth
rises up to meet the withering sun,
the ignorant sun that probes into
the wrinkle of the past and puts to sleep
the memories of night, the cruel sun that
kills even the life of forgetting.
Yet there is beauty even in cracked things.
There is the wonder of the open eye
and the clear head and the brave smile.
There is the amazing giddiness of child
after shattering of toys,
the joys of being alive, of putting
aside the revery, the hope, the calculation,

for the burst of lavender, the aged friend,
the inspiration.
The old house thrives in its decay,
for it has known a time of day
when kindred spirits walked its halls,
and it has nourished all their souls.
In this house there is no room
for those who would make talk of doom;
and if its walls go up in fire,
its last will be its finest hour.

Bible Study

Chapter VI

BRICKS AND MORTAR
(1964-1967)

1

The winds of change continued to blow. During the summer of 1964, three young organizers working on behalf of African-American voting rights in Mississippi were murdered by white segregationists in an escalation of the Civil Rights struggle. The Mississippi Summer broadened into a sweep of protests (on campuses and in society), by which the nation was ultimately changed. The University of Tennessee never experienced the widespread violence which erupted in many locations, but the era of upheaval had arrived in Knoxville.

In this environment of tumult, the fourth full-time director-campus minister began work at the Wesley Foundation in June 1964. Robert E. (Bob) Parrott, a Louisianian, had been campus minister at the University of Southwestern Louisiana (now the University of Louisiana at Lafayette) and Louisiana State University in Baton Rouge in the 1950s. He had attended Union Theological Seminary in New York, and for several years before coming to Knoxville, had done graduate work at Vanderbilt Divinity School in Nashville as the recipient of two Danforth Foundation Campus Ministry grants, while also pastor of two rural churches. Following the Supreme Court decision (*Brown v. Board of Education*), he had pioneered in desegregating the Wesley Foundation in Lafayette in August 1954, the earliest instance of a fully bi-racial state campus community in the Deep South.

THE SHINING OF LIGHT: A HISTORY OF THE WESLEY FOUNDATION
AT THE UNIVERSITY OF TENNESSEE, 1922-2007

Bob Parrott, 1964

Clearly, the immediate task at the UTK Wesley Foundation was three-fold -- to support and further develop the small student group, reduced in number but not in quality after the difficult academic year of 1963-1964; to re-build a relationship of trust with the Holston Conference and the three supporting Methodist Districts, particularly the Knoxville District, in addition to mending relationships with the University administration; and to re-activate the dormant plans for a new building at 1718 Melrose Place. Each of the goals was of importance. If the campus ministry was to survive, each goal needed urgent attention.

Interestingly, the first telephone call Bob received on his first day at the office, on June 11, 1964, came from a reporter from *The Knoxville Journal,* inquiring about the "program changes" envisioned after the "difficulties" of the previous year. The call foreshadowed the immediacy of the challenge facing the Wesley Foundation community, as well as the degree to which the student community was being closely monitored.

The house was in a state of majestic decay. Laughingly, students said, "The windows don't open and the doors don't close!" The stove in the kitchen allowed only one electric eye to be used at one time, for if two or more were utilized, the entire wiring system in the house often shorted out. There were plumbing and sewer-line problems. The shabby lounge furniture, most if it originally used in the house on Temple Avenue, needed urgent replacement. An inventory of furnishings made during the summer of 1964 included an RCA Victor television set "with rabbit ears," a "grand piano painted gray," a "mahogany dining table with a broken leg", a mahogany record player-radio combination, a ping-pong table, an LC Smith typewriter, a Corona adding machine, a mimeograph machine, two Westinghouse refrigerators, and a Coca-Cola machine. Before the beginning of the fall quarter, Bob and the students painted the back porch and the pantry; they cleaned the basement, and disposed of several years of accumulated junk.

The 1963-1964 Student Council had been reelected for 1964-1965, with Charles Fowler as president and Albert Wilhelm as vice-president. (Albert resigned in mid-year.) Beginning in Fall 1964, other active student leaders included Bettye Hall, Perk Thornton, Donna Blakely, Andy Petty, Augustus (Gus) Wilson, Cheryl Landgren, Ann Russell, Tommie Moore, Ruth Fox, Lucy Browder, Rosemary Hunter, Bill Baird, Samera Major, Jane Hembree, and David Houdeshell. Residents living on the third floor were Charles Fowler, Perk Thornton, Michael Rowe, Jim Reeves and Charles Reeves. Ronald Koo, a Hong-Kong student, lived in the makeshift room in the basement.

Students embarked on a study of the purpose of the Wesley Foundation, using *Witness to the Campus,* edited by Roger Ortmayer, and *Campus Evangelism* by Richard N. Bender as source materials. The study considered the reasons for the Wesley Foundation's presence on the campus and the reasons for the Wesley Foundation in the life of the church. The Council was reorganized, with new officers beginning in spring quarter 1965. Fellowship, retreats, Wednesday suppers and a lecture-discussion series were highlights; discussions included topics such as The

THE SHINING OF LIGHT: A HISTORY OF THE WESLEY FOUNDATION
AT THE UNIVERSITY OF TENNESSEE, 1922-2007

Civil Rights Act, a study of Christian art in Africa, and the fragmented character of the university society. There were Sunday Vespers in the Chapel and Wednesday evening Holy Communion. Thursday Luncheons were reorganized by combining a meal for students and faculty; the housekeeper-cook Carrie E. Johnson resigned, replaced by Ada P. Jones, whose delicious meals became a signature of the year. Thirteen delegates attended the Eighth Quadrennial MSM conference in Lincoln, Nebraska, December 28-January 2, 1964-1965. Students from Tyson House, the Presbyterian Center, Knoxville College and Wesley Foundation gathered for the observance of the Universal Day of Prayer.

The play, *Christ in the Concrete City,* was presented at the Foundation, and then was taken on tour to area churches as chancel productions. Players included Cheryl Landgren, Lucy Browder, Ann Russell, Sandra Jones, Tommie Moore, Charles Fowler, Albert Wilhelm, and Bill Baird. A new outreach program at Wesley House Community Center started, in which students engaged in painting, wall-building, and the improvement of playground facilities. A new mimeographed publication, *Wesley's Words,* was distributed weekly; another publication, *Campus,* was mailed regularly to supporting churches. During 1964-1965, Sunday Morning Worship in the Chapel and programmed participation in the Back Door Coffee-House did not continue.

Some students and faculty were sharply disappointed in the change of style and emphasis by the new director, a reminder that transitions in campus ministry can be difficult and painful, especially for those accustomed to established procedures. Three students expressed extreme displeasure with the programming and with the new atmosphere at 1718 Melrose Place which they characterized as "oppressive." Another student suggested that "the new regime" had set the Wesley Foundation back "at least 20 years."

BRICKS AND MORTAR
(1964-1967)

In his annual report entitled "A Campus Ministry in Mid-Passage" to the Board of Directors on February 26, 1965, the director emphasized the need for more adequate facilities. The concept of the Wesley Foundation offered as a "home away from home" was not stressed as a major goal of the ministry, but efforts then underway to build close Christian community in the old house were described and encouraged. Work to improve active relationships to local churches was in process. It was recommended that the Board's Building Committee should proceed "with vigor and conviction" toward providing new, adequate facilities for the ministry. The employment of a staff assistant was recommended. Staff commendations were made, on behalf of Pattie J. Cain, secretary, Ada P. Jones, housekeeper-cook, and particularly Charles Fowler, president of the Council, "who has offered outstanding leadership during a period of difficulty and change." Charles was elected president of the Tennessee State Methodist Student Movement in April 1965.

By historic motion, the Board (at its meeting on February 26, 1965) set in motion official planning for the new building, calling for a thoroughgoing re-study of the existing plans, and for a contract to be let in January 1966, the projected cost at $200,000, instead of the original figure of $190,000. It was anticipated that construction would begin in spring 1966. J. Preston Hess, head of the Building Committee, noted that the construction would coincide with the celebration of Knoxville Methodism's 150th anniversary. An audit report, dated May 31, 1965, showed $123,609 on certificates of deposit in the Building Fund, representing funds received sporadically since 1958.

On April 27, 1965, the Board approved the employment of Barbara Lyn Belcher, soon to graduate from Radford College in Virginia, as assistant director, at a salary of $375 per month. Barbara had been active in the student leadership at the Radford Wesley Foundation.

THE SHINING OF LIGHT: A HISTORY OF THE WESLEY FOUNDATION AT THE UNIVERSITY OF TENNESSEE, 1922-2007

By late spring 1965, many "last" events were occurring. The last Student Council members to operate in the old house were elected: Augustus (Gus) Wilson, president; Andrew Petty, vice-president; Donna Blakely, secretary; and Sara Rushing, treasurer. The last community of students to live in the old house was chosen, including Charles Fowler, Gus Wilson, Perk Thornton, Douglas Henry, Andy Petty, Fred Price and Ronald Koo. Others who moved in (during 1966) were Durwood Robinson, Don Dennis, Dewey Hodges and Bryan Warden. The last summer events and the last fall programming were planned. Among the students, there was excitement about the coming new building, but the continuing sadness -- that the old house had to be demolished in the process – pervaded many discussions.

Gus Wilson, president, in an issue of *Cross-Currents,* a new Wesley Foundation publication issued twice a quarter, wrote about the large numbers of students who were uninterested in the church, according to a national poll. "I do not think it means that we should attempt to recruit church members to save the church. Rather, I think we should try to create a meaningful and relevant relationship between the church and society. We can do this only by responding to the needs of society, and this we can do by what we plan, by being unafraid to try new ideas, such as new forms of worship, and by trying to find new ways of relating old traditions to our current situation....."

The death of Charles Barber, the architect who had drawn the original plans for a new structure, necessitated a new design by the Barber & McMurry firm, but before this new set could be drawn, in-depth conversations were begun to determine not only the physical shape of a new building but also a theology of campus ministry for the future. Form was to be determined by meaning. The decade of the 1960s was an age when many campus ministries questioned the value of maintaining expensive buildings, an idea highlighted by Thomas Oden, in the MSM study guide, *The*

BRICKS AND MORTAR
(1964-1967)

Community of Celebration. Oden characterized campus ministry buildings as ghettos for Christians at the periphery of the campus, and concluded that the point of such buildings was to keep the denominational faithful away from the distractions of the university. The Executive and Building Committees of the Board found Oden's conclusions not applicable to the UTK situation.

In retrospect, these summer 1965 conversations in the old Melrose Place house – many of them lasting until late in the evening – were highly significant for the future, and in the process a theology of campus ministry was debated, clarified and refocused. Clearly the building was *not* the ministry, yet the building should provide a base, a headquarters, an open locus for the life of the church on the campus, and should foster an accepting, inclusive, redemptive community of people – primarily students, but also faculty members and university staff – which worshipped, studied, worked in mission, and grew in grace. In short, the UTK Wesley Foundation was to be neither adjunct to a local church program nor a ghetto into which students could retreat, but the *full presence of the church on the university campus.* The ideas of J. Preston Hess were central in these conversations. Repeatedly, he stressed that the UTK Wesley Foundation was to be the witness of The Methodist Church on the university campus, and that the building and the ministry should give light, "like a beacon."

In the course of these discussions, Don Howden, one of the Barber & McMurry architects, asked Bob Parrott to draw his own architectural ideas for the new building; these ideas, sketched on several pages of lined yellow pads, were critiqued by the Building Committee. These sketches envisioned a comfortable lounge, an institutional kitchen, offices, a library, a large community room, small meeting rooms, a theatre, and a set of residence-hall rooms for a community of students who would serve as student staff for the ministry. (The concept of the student-staff rooms had slowly developed from the tradition of students living in various places in the houses at 908 Temple Avenue and 1718 Melrose Place.)

Don Howden then drew a new set of preliminary plans, which he presented to the Building and Executive Committees on October 25, 1965, and to the full Board on November 4. It was reported that anticipated income to be received by 1968 would likely result in $163,900 as a building reserve; the architect now estimated the building cost at $175,120, plus contractor's fee, architect's fees, furnishings and equipment, or approximately $236,600. The Board anticipated that a loan of $100,000 would be needed. (A fee of $3,000 had already been paid to the architectural firm for the earlier set of plans.) It was suggested that the facilities of the old house could be used through Winter Quarter of 1966, and that its demolition would likely begin in April 1966.

Another Barber & McMurry architect assumed the major role in designing and execution, replacing Don Howden – Robert C. Parrott (no relation to Robert E. Parrott the campus minister) began detailed work, and throughout the entire project the two Bob Parrotts worked closely together. (Coincidentally, both Bob Parrotts had become the fathers of sons born at Baptist Hospital in Knoxville on the same day, December 31, 1964.)

2

A major program feature of the "last year" in the old house was Dialogue, a Sunday evening meal-discussion, in which speakers and resource people presented opposing sides of current issues (e.g., on politics, the sexual revolution, the war in Vietnam, university policies, the military draft, criminal justice, etc.), in order to create a genuine dialogue in the audience, thus facilitating students in the development of their own perspectives. A Sunday morning seminar (from 9:15 to 10:30 a.m.) studied Leander E. Keck's *Taking the Bible Seriously,* its objective the historical-

BRICKS AND MORTAR
(1964-1967)

critical method of Bible study. Covenant communities studied Tillich's *Dynamics of Faith* and Bonhoeffer's *Letters and Papers from Prison*. A married students' program was coordinated by Tom Hood, a member of the Sociology faculty, and his wife Ginger Hood.

A memorable 1965 Christmas celebration was held in the old house, featuring a delicious meal cooked by Ada P. Jones, and a musical "extravaganza" prepared by students. During the preparation of the meal, all electrical power was lost for at least an hour. As soon as power was restored, water from an overflowing second floor toilet began flooding into the downstairs vestibule. To the end, maintaining everyday life in the house was a challenge.

The projected date for demolishing the old house (spring 1966) loomed in the immediate future. Since the existing Chapel could not be available for use during demolition and new construction, the Board and students were faced with the question of how the campus ministry was to operate in the interim, until fall 1967 or even winter 1968. Some Board members suggested that all activities be suspended, but students and the campus minister proposed a continuation of the ministry at a temporary site, even in cramped quarters, in order that the Foundation's organized presence on campus could continue. Consequently, on March 18, 1966, the Building Committee agreed to purchase the brick residence of Dr. and Mrs. James K. Bletner at 905 Mountcastle Street (facing Mountcastle Park on Lake Avenue, three blocks west of Melrose Place) for the price of $26,500. It was further arranged that the University would purchase the Bletner property from the Foundation when the new building was completed. The two-story residence had a living room, dining room, kitchen, three bedrooms and a rear apartment which could be utilized to house the ministry in its diaspora.

THE SHINING OF LIGHT: A HISTORY OF THE WESLEY FOUNDATION AT THE UNIVERSITY OF TENNESSEE, 1922-2007

Many problems presented themselves in the course of the new building's construction, and were mostly solved. For example, locating the building toward the rear of the Melrose Place lot, rather than at the front of the lot where the old house had been, was a wise decision, but it meant losing many ancient trees in the original back yard; the trees fell to progress as Mrs. Kulhman's azalea garden (at the site of the Chapel) had done in 1957. To avoid construction work, campus pedestrians increasingly utilized a narrow, shaded pathway beside the Chapel; the pathway became a not-so-secret place for the smoking of marijuana. The amount of paperwork during construction was enormous: the constant attention of Fred D. Loy, Board treasurer, was invaluable in monitoring and meeting construction payment deadlines.

In a mixture of elation and uncertainty, the energies of many people in April 1966 focused on moving out of the house at 1718 Melrose Place and moving into the cramped quarters at 905 Mountcastle Street. Some of the finest features of the Melrose Place house were sold – the grand walnut staircase in the front vestibule, the massive front door, the mullioned windows from the dining room, the leaded glass doors from the bookcases on the third floor, a few light fixtures, and even the rounded stones from the vestibule fireplace. The *Cantoria* plaster frieze above the living room fireplace was painstakingly removed and packed in sawdust, to be used in the new building.

The end of sixty years of house history began on May 16, 1966, when wrecking crews arrived. A crowd of students stood watching from across the street. Demolition was rapid. Within a few days, even most of the rubble was gone. There remained only a gigantic crater where the basement had been. (Bob Parrott climbed into the crater and rescued half a dozen original 1906-1907 bricks left from the house's foundation.) The Chapel stood at the top of the lot, its doors barricaded. An era had ended.

BRICKS AND MORTAR
(1964-1967)

The V.L. Nicholson Company was retained as the contractor. The borrowing of $150,000 was approved. A grand total of $313,000 was estimated as the total cost of the project.

When Barbara Belcher finished her year as assistant director, Margaret Anne Shanks was hired. With remarkable grace under pressure, Anne worked tirelessly in the difficult transition period between buildings, assisting in the adjustment to new surroundings and maintaining a remarkable level of ministry. New Council leadership included Charles Mitchell, president; Cheryl Landgren, vice-president; Corinne Varner, secretary; and Don Dennis, treasurer. Remarkably, a full program of activities, meals and student residents was maintained in the crowded spaces in the Mountcastle house; during living room discussions and programs, students sat on the stairway and on the floor, for lack of seating space. Occasionally they stood on the side screened porch and listened to speakers through the open door. Ada Jones and the student residents managed to use the same small kitchen simultaneously. The improvised conditions finally evoked a growing excitement. Living in the bedrooms and the adjoining apartment were Randall Bass, Mike Wright, Don Dennis, Leonard Gucwa, Vance Archer and Kenton Dickerson. Other active leaders included Victor McCauley, Margaret Colditz, Jack Greer, Gay Morgan, James Harris, James Stockton, Nancy Rundle, Tay Ward, Sandra Lee Waters, Vance Sherwood, and Kay Fory.

Reminiscent of the meditation chapel built in the basement of the Temple Avenue house, students improvised a small space as a chapel in the basement of the Mountcastle house, and named it "The Catacombs." They sometimes used paper nametags in the shape of a fish (*ichthus*) to symbolize their community in exile.

On Sunday, October 30, 1966 at 4:00 p.m., a service of ground breaking was held at the 1718 Melrose Place site, near the large crater created by the demolition. Students Victor McCauley

THE SHINING OF LIGHT: A HISTORY OF THE WESLEY FOUNDATION
AT THE UNIVERSITY OF TENNESSEE, 1922-2007

Tuesday, Nov. 1, 1966

DIRTY WORK — Helping with the groundbreaking ceremony for the new Wesley Foundation, Sunday, are the Rev. Robert E. Parrot, campus minister; Victor McCauley, Murfreesboro freshman; and Ronald Yu-Lin Koo, graduate student.

Ground Broken Sunday For Wesley Foundation

Ground breaking, October 30, 1966

BRICKS AND MORTAR
(1964-1967)

and Ronald Yu-Lin Koo helped Bob Parrott turn the first spade of earth. Others participating were Board president Dr. Neal Peacock and the University's executive dean of student affairs Dr. Charles L. Lewis. J. Preston Hess, chairman of the Building Committee, and Dr. F. Heisse Johnson, director of the Holston Conference office of Christian Higher Education, were present. An article in *The Knoxville News-Sentinel* summarized Dr. Peacock's remarks, noting "...A great university and a dynamic church have much in common; both are dedicated to truth. Students have found a partnership with the University and the Church." Bob Parrott was disappointed that few students attended the event.

905 Mountcastle Street, Knoxville
Kenton Dickerson

3

Assistant Director Anne Shanks concluded her work at the Foundation in spring 1967. She and Arthur (Art) Miller were married in the Melrose Place Chapel in June 1967, the first wedding celebrated there during construction. Connection to the new building had been made with a new narthex, which served both Chapel and Theatre.

The new building took shape rapidly. The Parrott children, 5-year-old Leslie and 2-year-old Crit, enjoyed coming with their father to the construction site, where they played in the unfinished Community Room and in the long central hallway. During the summer of 1967, while Ott Ellis served as summer president, students refinished some of the existing pieces of the old Temple Avenue furniture. The top of the mahogany dining table was resurfaced and fitted to a new wrought iron base. Old file cabinets were repaired; old folding chairs were painted orange. The screened porch of the Mountcastle house became a repair shop. New furnishings for the new building were purchased. Donna Parrott and Tacie Peacock co-chaired the committee for furnishing the new Lounge, working with Terry Fielden, interior decorator. New residential furniture was ordered. Ada Jones supervised the installation of equipment in the new kitchen, the central gas range (with double ovens) her pride and joy. Among the students there was finally an air of excited disbelief about the coming move back to 1718 Melrose Place. The Wesley Foundation's original journey of 24 years since the first Center had been occupied had been a long one.

The new building, bright and shining and spacious, was ready. In the first days of the fall term, the move from Mountcastle Street back to Melrose Place was accomplished. On September 23, 1967, the finished structure was opened officially to the public. The total cost, including landscaping, equipment and new furnishings, was $325,000, an increase of $89,000 more than projected approximately a year earlier. However, the amount of the 20-year loan, negotiated through Hamilton National Bank in Johnson City, TN at 6% interest, had been maintained at $150,000, repayable annually at $12,500 or $6,250 every six-months.

BRICKS AND MORTAR
(1964-1967)

Page 2 The Knoxville News-Sentinel Saturday, September, 23, 1967

U-T Wesley Foundation To Expand
New $285,000 Building Opens on Campus

By ALICE M. SMITH
News-Sentinel Church Editor

The new melon-colored brick, $285,000 U-T Wesley Foundation opened its doors for the first time last night with an informal open house, marking the beginning of a school year that will see new lines of emphasis by the foundation in its campus ministry.

"We're really trying to expand our ministry to include the whole university, rather than just the undergraduates," said Rev. Robert E. Parrott, director. "We want to get away from the image of just being a Methodist student center." The foundation building is at 1718 Melrose Place.

"This building will not only be for Methodists but for all of U-T," he said. "For instance, we will encourage the faculty and other groups to make use of our facilities for such things as seminars and dramas."

Emphasize Small Groups

Mr. Parrott said there will be more emphasis on small groups, "instead of one large mass. Here at U-T where classes are often large, one of the great values of these religious centers is for people to find personal identity and personal relationships that are meaningful.

"Under our study curriculum, we have seven small groups of not more than 12 which meet weekly for study, discussion, work projects and community involvement."

Mr. Parrott said there will still be large group meetings such as the Sunday night fellowships, including a supper at 5:30 p.m. followed by a discussion period called "dialogue." "We talk about anything of interest—morality, ethics, the nature of U-T, the sexual revolution, the war in Vietnam," said Mr. Parrott.

JUST FINISHED — This is the $285,000 U-T Wesley Foundation plant which went into use last night with an open house for University students. Sweeping the sidewalk in preparation for the party, from left, are Vance Archer, Nashville, president of the organization, Lenny Gucwa, vice president, and Rev. Robert Parrott, director.

The new building opens,
September 23, 1967

There were a few glitches in the readiness for the opening day: the carpet ordered for the Lounge had been improperly measured, and a large square space of paint-spattered concrete floor showed; several weeks elapsed before the additional carpet was laid.

All the new residential furniture had not arrived. The old black and white television set positioned in the Community Room suddenly died a noble death. Acoustics in the new Theatre were poor, and fiberglass panels, covered in burlap, were yet to be installed to soak up sound. But it was a gloriously sunny day -- a fitting metaphor for the shining of light – in celebration of a dream long dreamed. Townspeople and students wandered through the new facility and were amazed – they pronounced it "wonderful."

On that day, Dr. Neal Peacock planted a young magnolia tree on the front lawn, a symbol of the new beginning. The tree still flourishes.

NEARING COMPLETION — The $315,000 addition to University of Tennessee's Wesley Foundation building is nearing completion, and officials hope to occupy it by fall quarter. It adjoins the chapel at 1718 Melrose Place completed in 1958. The structure, to be one of the most complete of its kind anywhere, is being built by V. L. Nicholson Co. Architect was Barber and McMurry. Rev. Robert E. Parrott is campus minister of the organization, sponsored by Holston Conference of the Methodist Church.

Almost Finished

Chapter VII

BEING THE CHURCH
(1967-1977)

1

Developing a new ministry utilizing the new building was full of "firsts", challenges and problems. On January 7, 1968, Sunday Morning Worship was re-instituted, announced as "an integral part of the mission of the Wesley Foundation." These services at 10:45 a.m. were not in competition with worship in surrounding local churches, but were an additional opportunity offered to the thousands of students in residence halls who were within easy walking distance of the building. The new services were announced in the *Orange and White* and on-campus billboards throughout the fall quarter 1967. The decision was made to use the new Theatre instead of the Chapel which could seat only approximately sixty people comfortably. The beginning attendance was approximately 75. A coffee-hour was held in the Community Room on the main floor beginning at 10:15 a.m. In the Theatre, the new yellow chairs were set in a semi-circular arrangement around the altar, behind which hung a handmade banner declaring "God Is With Us." Student liturgists and musicians presided at the service; the campus minister was usually the preacher. The first sermon was entitled "The Creative Peril of Honest Doubt," but soon students were often sharing the Morning Word in a sequence of three mini-sermons on a coordinated topic.

Thursday Luncheon was expanded, beginning in fall 1967, creating a non-programmed fellowship meal designed for the entire campus community, served from 11:30 a.m. to 1:00 p.m., with

Theatre worship, ca 1968

meals prepared by Ada Jones. A favorite menu was Italian lasagna, green salad and French bread, iced tea and coffee. In order to develop lively conversation, students were encouraged to invite their professors and teaching assistants to lunch. At the time, it was one of the few events on campus where students, faculty, and staff sat together at the same tables for a relaxed meal. Thursday Luncheon became a campus tradition; many people were introduced to the campus ministry through this meal. As early as fall 1967, the attendance at Thursday Luncheon was approximately 125.

Pattie Jenkins Cain, the Wesley Foundation secretary since 1963, had presided over an office in a converted bedroom in the old house, had assisted in the move to Mountcastle Street and then had re-established the new office in the new building. Her resignation was received with many expressions of appreciation by the Board, the campus minister and students. She had been a valuable part of the ministry. A new secretary, Jackie H. Bauguss, was hired.

The first head resident couple, who coordinated the residential community and served as official "night time" hosts, were William C. (Bill) Aiken and his wife Juanita (Nita). The first residents were Randall Bass, Donald Dennis, Choo-Hua Jonah Eng, David E. Walker, Leonard Gucwa, Stephen Stout, Vance Archer, James Paul Welker, and Fred Wyatt. The concept of the "Community Fellow" program centered on the presence of a "student staff" who shared basic building tasks and formed their own version of Christian community.

The 1967-1968 Student Council was led by Vance Archer, president; Donald Dennis and Leonard Gucwa, vice-presidents; Jacque Arnold and Donna Cheaney, secretaries, and Arthur (Ott) Ellis, treasurer. A weekly program of small group discussions, Wednesday Vespers in the Chapel, Sunday Supper-and-Dialogue continued. On January 14, 1968, Dr. William L. Thomas "dialogued" on "University Housing and Student Life." On January 28, the Dialogue topic was "Cheating and the Honor System," with a panel of seven faculty and university staff members. Although the national MSM was losing ground in an effort to support the ecumenical movement, the Tennessee State MSM was still vital; the February 1968 meeting in Cookeville was concerned with the topic, "Situational Ethics and Beyond." There were monthly Student-Faculty Luncheons: on February 12, the announced theme was "The Search for Meaning and Values: Is the Academic Process Concerned?" Other active students in 1967-1968 were Gene Cash, Bonnie Frerichs, Jo Ann Fisher, Corinne Varner, Mary Crippen, Fred Binkley, Charles Coffee, Dewey Hodges, Martha Sue Polk, Suzette Stevenson, and Charlotte Babcock.

THE SHINING OF LIGHT: A HISTORY OF THE WESLEY FOUNDATION
AT THE UNIVERSITY OF TENNESSEE, 1922-2007

The Wesley Foundation Board decided to sell the Alta Vista Way parsonage and to offer the campus minister a housing allowance instead.

In response to the newly published report, *A Study of Wesley Foundations and the Campus Ministry* by Samuel N. Gibson, the Board implemented a self-study, in which there was a critical analysis of the program, the residential community, current issues on the UTK campus, and the MSM and the University Christian Movement. Board member Dr G. Pedro Smith was instrumental in assisting the Student Council to begin its own process of self-evaluation. Responses from Council members were submitted, including the following: ".....The emphasis of Wesley Foundation programming should be both Christian experience and service. We must consider to whom we are directing our program. Are we mainly ministering to those who already experience Christ in their lives or do we reach out those who have not known Him? A ministry that reaches all must provide religious experience, Christian service and experiences that introduce Christianity to those who are not yet serious or interested in living Christ-like lives." In the age of rising student power, students rightly sought a greater share in determining the shape and direction of the Foundation's ministry.

The next Council president, Ott Ellis, was elected to begin a new term in spring 1968. Judy Colditz and J'Lain Norris served as vice-presidents. Martha Sue Polk was secretary, and Fred Wyatt was treasurer. Other active student leaders were Carroll Varner, Emily Warlick, Jeanette Collins and David Walker. The 1968-1969 residential community included Charles Coffey, Roy Holder, Joe Huber, William Nicholson, Darrell Powell, Joe Bishop, William C. Reed, Derrick Snider, James Paul Welker, and Fred Wyatt. A new Council theme was developed: "CRUCIAL: Christian Responsibility in the University Community and In All Life."

BEING THE CHURCH
(1967-1977)

In fall 1968, the staff arrangement was re-organized, during which Yugo Suzuki, a recent seminary graduate of Japanese ancestry, was named Assistant Director and Head Resident; he and his wife Elizabeth occupied the ground floor apartment. The quiet, scholarly Suzukis added an admired presence within the Wesley Foundation. Anne Shanks Miller continued on the staff until spring 1969, at which time Elizabeth Suzuki assumed her position. Anne Shanks Miller was long remembered as a steady, effective friend of many students.

The first African-American student joined the residential community in fall 1969 – James Melvin Washington, a Baptist minister who was also attached to the staff of a leading black Baptist church in Knoxville. James' affability and intelligence made him a popular favorite among Wesley Foundation students. Other residents were Michael Cameron, Robert Hall, Tom Handwerker, Roy Holder, Lynn Hoskins, Joe Huber, Michael Lusk, Tom Scalf, Lynn Sheeley, and David Walker. Elected officers serving on the Student Council included David Walker, president; Bonnie Frerichs, vice-president; Sylvane (Sunny) Griffith, secretary; and Michael Cameron, treasurer.

1970 was a climactic year of campus protests and student activism. A larger student role in decision-making at UTK was demanded. Demonstrations against the hiring of Edward J. Boling as president of the university gained nationwide attention. Anti-Vietnam War sentiment was strong and vocal, and large noontime rallies in Circle Park could be organized in a few hours' time. There was a daily climate of agitation and confrontation. (The Wesley Foundation received several telephone threats that the building was about to be seized and "occupied" by demonstrating groups, but no occupation ever occurred; it also received two bomb threats.) The rioting and deaths at Kent State University further fueled the Knoxville fire. In May 1970, there was a three-day campus strike; classes were declared voluntary, not mandatory.

THE SHINING OF LIGHT: A HISTORY OF THE WESLEY FOUNDATION AT THE UNIVERSITY OF TENNESSEE, 1922-2007

The volatile spring of 1970 climaxed in Neyland Stadium at a Billy Graham Crusade before a capacity crowd of 75,000 people, at which time President Richard Nixon was introduced as a special guest, his first public appearance since base camps in Cambodia had been attacked by American forces in an escalation of the Vietnam War. Among the attending crowd and on the field there were protests and disruptions – a group of students and faculty members bearing anti-war signs was arrested, charged with "disturbing public worship." Campus security personnel took photographs of other students in the stands, purportedly shouting obscenities at the president. Among those students photographed was Foundation resident James Washington. When James returned to the Foundation building later that evening, he told Bob Parrott that because of the photograph he might be arrested. He had not been shouting obscenities at the president, he said, but had been photographed with his mouth open!

The next day, Knoxville police arrived at the Foundation and arrested James, who was taken directly to jail. Bob Parrott and a group of students arranged his bail; James was released. After several months, charges against him were dropped. He graduated from UTK with high honors, and later received advanced degrees from Yale University, including a Ph.D. degree in church history. As an author and distinguished professor at Union Theological Seminary in New York, he became one of the nation's authorities on African-American history. One of his major works was to edit the writings of Martin Luther King, Jr., published as *A Testament of Hope: The Essential Writings and Speeches of Martin Luther King, Jr.* in 1990. In 1995, he published *Conversations with God: Two Centuries of Prayers by African-Africans.* James died of hypertensive stroke on May 3, 1997 at the age of 49.

BEING THE CHURCH
(1967-1977)

2

Neal D. Peacock concluded his presidency of the Wesley Foundation Board in spring 1970, having served on the Board with distinction since its beginning in 1957. As a churchman and a respected academician, his influence on the Foundation has become indelible, marked by generosity, efficiency and wisdom. He, J. Preston Hess and J. Wesley Hoffmann became honorary members of the Board. The new Board president was Dr. O. Glen Hall, dean of the College of Agriculture.

By early spring 1970, a severe and lengthy financial crisis developed, the first of many such dilemmas in the years following the construction of the new building. As a result, there was difficulty in paying the $6250 semi-annual mortgage payments. For the first time, a few of these payments were made a few days late. The position of Associate Campus Minister was deleted from the staff, and stringent cut-backs in spending were made. The deepening crisis continued until 1972, during which time a few members of the Board and others wondered whether the campus ministry would survive.

Within this crisis, an arrangement developed whereby the Lutheran Campus Ministry utilized the Chapel for Sunday Morning Worship at 9:45 a.m., while Foundation worship was held in the Theatre at 11:00 a.m., with a joint coffee hour in the Conference Room beginning at 9:15 a.m. The Lutheran campus pastor, Joseph (Joe) Meixner, known to his students as "Pastor Joe," soon established an office at the Foundation, and several cooperative projects developed, including Sunday evening meals and Encounters. Lutherans contributed a beginning monthly amount of $130 to the Foundation's budget. Although a few Wesley Foundation students found the cooperation awkward, the arrangement worked well, and continued for several years; Joe Meixner was followed by pastor William (Bill) Couch.

THE SHINING OF LIGHT: A HISTORY OF THE WESLEY FOUNDATION AT THE UNIVERSITY OF TENNESSEE, 1922-2007

Consideration was given to the possibility of a joint United Methodist-Lutheran appointment of an Associate Campus Minister whose responsibility would be work in residence halls, in the international student community, and on the campus at large. This idea never materialized.

Another self-study of campus ministry developed in 1971, this one involving Episcopalians, Presbyterians and United Methodists, directed by a local campus committee using guidelines from United Ministries in Higher Education (UMHE), a consortium of denominational groups. David Dungan, UTK professor of Religious Studies, served as chairperson; the UMHE regional representative was Clyde Robinson. Aimed at investigating the possibilities of significant joint cooperation between the Boards of the three groups, a series of meetings, interviews, and consultations proceeded for almost nine months. The final report from the UMHE Self-Study Committee was received by the Foundation's Executive Committee on February 10, 1972; Neal Peacock and a sub-committee were asked to prepare a summary of the findings to be distributed to the full Board. Dr. Peacock termed the report "challenging, provocative.....and worthy of consideration." He further responded by saying that several items could be easily misunderstood, and that Board members were likely to be "put on the defensive" by the findings.

The UMHE perspective concluded that the three campus ministries were not coordinated effectively and acted independently of one another. The ministries were also found to be "too centered in buildings," and were not involved in residence halls, fraternity houses, in faculty and administration offices, and in the offices of the city of Knoxville. UMHE guidelines declared that the significance of higher education was to help shape the future of society through teaching, research and public service, and that ministry in higher education was to be a shared ministry of local churches and on-campus ministry. UMHE principles emphasized campus ministry as a ministry of the laity, with multiple styles and approaches. The Boards of the three ministries should be more than advisory groups, it said – Boards should share with the staffs in the development of strategies of ministry. A movement toward the formation of one joint Board supervising the three campus ministries (in the discussions, sometimes referred to as a "superstructure Board") was believed by many to be the aim of the self-study.

Clyde Robinson met extensively with the three campus ministers. By January 1972, he had concluded (in correspondence) that the three Boards were not taking the university seriously as a social institution; rather, the university was being treated as a collection of persons to be dealt with individually rather than a system "with a special purpose in and impact upon society." Clyde found little theological clarity among the campus ministers, a situation which was judged to be "debilitating." He emphasized repeatedly that there was no struggle for theological consensus at work among the campus ministers. He judged that the Boards were understood primarily as channels to their local churches "for financial and interpretive or political purposes, and for setting permissible parameters for the campus ministers." Church fragmentation was found to be "scandalous." He urged that efforts should be made to "pull the church together" to minister to the University as an institution, as well as to the people whose lives were touched by the University. He hoped that the self-study could be continued, and that specific recommendations would be made to the respective Boards.

The local self-study Committee, meeting for the last time on March 28, 1972, re-interpreted the UMHE recommendations. In short, it suggested that the three interested groups (hopefully with the addition of others, including Lutheran, Baptist and Roman Catholic Centers) organize future joint *coordinating efforts,* but that these efforts should not be construed as the first step toward the *"final organizational merger"* suggested by the UMHE report.

Within the Wesley Foundation Board, Glen Hall presided over lively and vigorous consideration of the UMHE guidelines and the final local report. Some voices found it helpful and creative; others concluded that the UMHE direction was "canned" and not suitable for the UTK campus. There was general consensus that any future movement toward a "joint Board" would require Holston Conference approval.

In response to the study, Board members of the three Boards met for a lively conference, "Student Christian Centers' Conference on Research" in Gatlinburg on April 13-14, 1973 with a declared objective – to "begin to understand some of the main intellectual currents of university life, specifically some of the moral and religious dilemmas posed by its quest for new knowledge, and to seek to find ways the Christian Centers might become relevant to this aspect of the university." Guest speakers were Dr. Mary Rose Gram, Dr. Henry Fribourg and Dr. George Schweitzer. After this meeting, however, the joint conversations did not officially continue.

In the midst of the Self-Study Committee's work, Bob Parrott reported (in "A Personal Letter to the Board, in Lieu of an Annual Report") that he was troubled both by the weaknesses of the Foundation's ministry and by his own inadequacies. He emphasized his frustration that he could not do *more* in the wider world of the University – e.g., in residence halls, in fraternity houses, and in relationships with faculty. He felt rightly and severely judged by the findings of the UMHE guidelines. Yet he maintained that the *development of Christian community* (a primary focus of his work) was essential to campus ministry. "I am convinced that the only true priority for campus ministry is the *enfleshment* of the servant Church in the university setting…..The force of a servant Church on a university campus means a painful struggle with the very heart of the Great Commandment..... I am concerned that the university be enabled to be the university, but at the same time I am concerned that the Church must be enfleshed to be the servant Church. I believe that the latter concern is the more central to our task."

In the same report, he related what had been a recent, meaningful celebration of Christian worship, during a sequence of three mini-sermons by three students on the topics, "Who is the Good Person? Who is the Religious Person? Who is the Christian Person?" In this series, a graduate student in chemistry (Cynthia Daugherty) made a moving plea for a singleness of purpose about *being religious.* She said that to be fully religious was not to say pious words and to do pious things but to give the fullness of mind and heart and energy to whatever task *really* counts ultimately in life. The report to the Board concluded, "The task that really counts here, I think, is to enflesh and celebrate Christ's mission – to love God with everything we've got, and to love our neighbor as ourselves. I believe that says it all."

3

One of the collateral results of the UMHE study was the formation of the Campus Ministers' Council (CMC), replacing an earlier more informal group which had met occasionally. The CMC was a collegial group comprised of full-time professional UTK chaplains who worked in the settings of established Centers. Through the Council a variety of cooperative, intra-Center efforts was developed, but the movement toward a cooperative ("superstructure") Board was never launched. Active in the CMC were the Disciples of Christ, the Church of Christ, Tyson House, the BSU, the Presbyterians, John XXIII Catholic Center, the Lutherans and the United Methodists. The CMC was recognized officially by the University as the "voice" representing campus religious concerns. Throughout at least 15 years or more, the CMC met regularly with representatives of the University administration (the Dean of Students, later the Dean of Student Affairs, plus representatives of the Office of Housing and the Student Counselling Center) and on occasions the University president. At least by the beginning of the 1970s, parachurch groups (such as Intervarsity, The Navigators, Campus Crusade for Christ and others) were organized, but did not initially gain membership in the CMC.

As an expression of the rise of student power and the appropriate demands of students for a greater share in decision-making at the Wesley Foundation, the Student Council was reorganized into the Coordinating Cabinet in the early 1970s, signaling a healthy attempt to represent a wider range of interests, concerns and on-campus involvement. Within the Cabinet were clearly identifiable areas of work (e.g., Worship, Foods, Finance, Community Involvement, Ecumenical Concerns, Publications, Fellowship Encounter, etc.) headed by an "area-head" (laughingly referred to as an "air-head") which operated independently but were coordinated by the whole, and presided over by its elected officers. The Coordinating Cabinet never functioned at its full potential, but it came closer than previous structures to expressing the larger goals of ministry and also *the leadership of the laity*. Students accepted a more responsible role in shaping the Church.

William (Bill) Neese and his wife Susan became the head resident couple in fall 1970; the residents were William Bryan, David Doan, William Doan, David Franklin, Kenneth Glass, Randall Lantz and Derrick Snider. And for the first time, two women students joined the residential community – Janet Sledge and Martelia (Marty) Miner. Leadership for the new Coordinating Cabinet in 1970-1971 was provided by Tom Handwerker. Other student leadership included Charlotte Behm, Harriet Behm, Lynda Durisko, Randall Lantz, Sylvane (Sunny) Griffith, James Johnston,

BEING THE CHURCH
(1967-1977)

Brenda Gardenhire, Bill Larzelere, Mary Ann Phifer, Jim Everhart, Jim Dedman and Lynn Hoskins. Sunday Morning Worship experimented with contemporary and folk services. There were dialogue sermons (one with Sister Bernadette Counihan and Bob Parrott on "The Uses and Misuses of Discipline") and a "visualized sermon" utilizing Saul Bellow's novel, *Herzog*. Sandy Mack, a professional folk singer and guitarist, participated in both Lutheran and Wesley Foundation services; she also sang at a Thanksgiving Dinner on November 21, 1970.

Gary Dunavant served as summer president in 1971, succeeded by Bill Larzelere for the academic year 1971-1972. On May 23, 1972, the year's ministry was reported on by students in the spring meeting of the Board of Directors. Highlighted were retreats at Camp Wesley Woods, a tutoring program at Wesley House Community Center, Thursday Student-Faculty Luncheons, the New Blood program, Sunday Night Supper and Encounter, and Sunday Worship in the Theatre with an attendance of approximately 100. To the Board, Bill Larzelere described "an exceptional Cabinet which showed much experience and stability." Other students reporting were Dennis Meaker, Robin Popp, Susan Gail Miller and Bryan K. Crow. In addition, area-heads were Carolyn Porter, Linda Martin, Nancy Hall, Robert McNeil, Kent Rowland and Bryan Crow.

Long remembered in early winter 1972 was a multi-media presentation prepared by the Fellow community entitled "But Most of All Wesley Is People," attempting to define the ministry and to illustrate its effect on students. The presentation utilized the then-popular song by Barbra Streisand, "People," and another popular refrain, "He Ain't Heavy, He's My Brother." A definition of the Wesley Foundation was expressed by Cabinet president Bill Larzelere in an open letter to on-campus students, "…..the Wesley Foundation, first of all, is a religious center on campus, but it is a unique one. Its entire program, all its activities are decided upon by students....."

The financial crisis had eased sufficiently by mid-year 1972 that the Board of Directors approved the addition of an associate campus minister to the staff. William E. (Bill) Nickle had been Associate Minister for Youth and Young Adults at Broad Street United Methodist Church in Kingsport, Tennessee, and brought many gifts to the Foundation – a unique blend of gentleness and a fierce passion for social justice. Bill's work largely involved on-campus and area activities – Law School forums, the Knoxville Urban Ministry, the Legal Aid Clinic and the Fort Sanders Tenants' Association.

By fall 1972, anti-Vietnam War fervor had diminished, but certainly had not disappeared. A speaker at a Sunday Night Encounter announced, "The day of the campus radical is coming to an end," but some people at the Wesley Foundation and some people on the UTK campus sharply disagreed. Those active in the Wesley Foundation represented the dichotomy. Generalized campus views toward the Foundation were also varied: some students considered it too "conservative," while others perceived it as far too "liberal."

The Coordinating Cabinet was led by Dennis Meaker in 1972-1973; other student leaders were Bryan Crow, Linda Martin, Donna McCorkle, Robert McNeil, Sherry Crouch, John Goins, Susan Miller, Nancy Hall, Kent Rowland and Robin Popp. Thomas W. (Tom) Parks became the head resident in the fall of 1972. This year the community of resident Fellows again included women students – Diana Abernathy, Sara Harville, Susan Miller and Mary (Penny) Boyd. Grant Ashley, Larry Garner, Charles Johnson, Randall Lantz, Bill Larzelere and Dennis Meaker were the men residents. Attendance at Sunday Morning Worship was approximately 125. Cooperative Wesley Foundation-Lutheran

BEING THE CHURCH
(1967-1977)

Encounters featured a series entitled "The Honest Shape of the Real World." The tutoring program at Wesley House involved 50 students working with 2nd through 6th graders. By spring 1973, the New Blood program had transported students to University Hospital to donate blood on behalf of those who could not afford the cost of $50 per pint. A highlight of winter 1973 was a "Black Arts Festival," a lively, crowded celebration featuring art and drama by UTK African-American students as well as a visiting group from Delaware State College, Dover, Delaware.

Through the years, many types of publications were utilized to introduce the Wesley Foundation to in-coming students. One of the most creative was "Bridges: A Photographic Interpretation of the Ministry of the University of Tennessee Wesley Foundation" in fall 1973, compiled and photographed by Bryan K. Crow, Cabinet president for the year 1973-1974. In its introduction was the following word: "The University of Tennessee Wesley Foundation builds bridges! Its campus ministry crosses some rivers which glint with joy and laughter, and spans others which run swiftly with despair. Some bridges sway in the winds of change.....We are struggling with the meaning of the deeper self and the wider world, and we are responding to the daily presence of God. And in its engineering, there are failures. But daily bridge-building continues, for this is the very nature of the Church at work and worship." Photographs showed the diversity of the Foundation's ministry – in discussion, meals, worship, at play, in community work, on retreats, all of it exemplified by student lay leadership. Featured were Susan Miller, Linda Martin, Randall Lantz, Suzanne Jackson, Martha Dalton, Mary Kay Buchanan, Robert Patterson, Robert McNeil, Debbie Freeland and others. The signature photograph showed a group of students crossing the plank footbridge at Camp Wesley Woods in early spring, on the journey, and the figure of a lone student (Robert Patterson) crossing it in solitude.

THE SHINING OF LIGHT: A HISTORY OF THE WESLEY FOUNDATION
AT THE UNIVERSITY OF TENNESSEE, 1922-2007

'Bridges'
Bryan K. Crow, photographer

BEING THE CHURCH
(1967-1977)

Another head resident couple, Gary and Linda Maas, began their work in fall 1973. The student residential community for the year included Thomas Bryan, Joanna (Jody) Buis, Karen Cromer, Jeannie Rybolt, Bryan Crow, Martha Dalton, Gay McDavid, Suzanne Jackson and Keith Hall. A significant addition to the community was Kleide Marcia Barbosa Alves, a Brazilian graduate student who arrived at UTK speaking limited English, and who within a few months was amazingly fluent. Like James Washington, Kleide made a remarkable impact on many fellow students. Today, as an Ed.D. professor of school psychology in Brazil, she also teaches in a theological seminary.

The years 1974-1976 were marked by strong Coordinating Cabinet leadership from Robert Patterson, succeeded by Mary Kay Buchanan. (Robert and Mary Kay were married in March 1979.)

On Retreat at Camp Wesley Woods

THE SHINING OF LIGHT: A HISTORY OF THE WESLEY FOUNDATION
AT THE UNIVERSITY OF TENNESSEE, 1922-2007

The residential community for 1974-1975 included Kleide Alves, Bryan Crow, Mike Kitchens, James Mathews, Marian Poindexter, Danny Armstrong, Stephen Campbell, Gwendolyn Harville and Thomas Hobbs. Alan Cornelius became the head resident in summer 1975. Fellows in 1975-1976 were Paula DePew, George Eckel, Thomas Jones, Gary Lipsomb, David Malone, Gay McDavid, Kathy Mitchell, Robert Patterson, Patricia Preston, James Webster and Philip Pingchu Young.

During these years, experimental forms of worship continued, featuring liturgical dance, film, student mini-sermons, and a wide variety of musical accompaniment. Robert Patterson led a choir, "Sunshine," whose regular members included Mary Kay Buchanan, Sally Zimmerman, Beverly Simmons, Teresa Adkins, Nancy Miller, Paula DePew, Julie Patterson, Carol Brown, Kathy Mitchell, JoAnn Creger, Gayle Pierson, Carol Hale, Paul Wright, Philip Young, Andy Tucker, Eddie Moore, Alan Cornelius and Lea Ousley. Bob Parrott experimented with "different" sermon contexts; the Service of the Word included sermon titles such as "God's Subtler Disguises," "You Make Me Believe in God," "Seeds Are For Planting" and "Okay! Now What Do You Do With Your Faith?" A popular guest speaker for Sunday Evening Encounters and Lenten Vespers was Dr. Jack Reese, president of the University. The Coordinating Cabinet was re-grouped into five major areas of work: Fellowship, Service, Communications, Issues/Study and Worship.

Bryan A. Jackson became the head resident in summer 1976. Residents for the 1976-1977 academic year were Alan McNabb, Sharon Kay Ray, Earl Sheridan, Beverly Ann Simmons, Anthony (Andy) Tucker, Elizabeth (Beth) Widner and Mary Kay Buchanan. Paul Wright served as president of the Coordinating Cabinet. Other student leaders included Danny Armstrong, Van Baxter, Suzanne Hooker, Gayle Pierson, Wally Wood, Andy Meacham, Suszie French, Julie Patterson and Sally Zimmerman.

BEING THE CHURCH
(1967-1977)

Frank M. (Bob) Bostick) was president of the Board of Directors; David E. Walker was treasurer. The perennial problem of greater involvement of District, faculty and ex-officio Board members in the on-going ministry was a recurring topic at Board meetings, as was the need for an "evaluation-study" of the campus ministry, which was soon mandated by the Holston Conference Board of Higher Education, and led by Dr. Edgar Eldridge, pastor of the Fountain City United Methodist Church. Methodists are perennially known for pulling up their roots to determine how they are growing.

The time was ripe for an audacious experiment in the mission of the Church.

NEWEST CENTER—This building at 1718 Melrose Avenue, houses the Wesley Foundation Methodist University Center on the University of Tennessee campus. The center was built by funds from the Holston Area of the United Methodist Church and is intended for the whole university community—students, faculty, staff—and, as such, is a locus for study, worship, inter-personal and group relationships.

Bright and Shining

THE SHINING OF LIGHT: A HISTORY OF THE WESLEY FOUNDATION
AT THE UNIVERSITY OF TENNESSEE, 1922-2007

Candle Lighting

Chapter VIII

STARS OVER SANTA CRUZ MIXTEPEC
(1977-1982)

1

The Wesley Foundation's 6-year mission in the Oaxaca region of southern Mexico, 1977-1982, changed and deepened the struggle to be the Church on campus in Knoxville. *Operation Mixtec: A World Hunger Project* began when Bob Parrott and John Wright, the UTK Presbyterian campus minister, met Tom Ibach, a missionary-paramedic who lived part-time in Chattanooga and part-time in a remote Mixtec Indian village in the Southern Sierra Madre Mountains in Mexico. In early 1977, Tom commuted to the Knoxville campus from Chattanooga several days a week, taking classes in anthropology. In conversations with Tom, the two campus ministers learned of his work among the Mixtecs, an indigenous people who had settled in the Southern Sierra Madres in the 16th century, contemporaries of the Toltecs and the Aztecs. In the village of Santa Cruz Mixtepec, Tom operated a medical clinic and worked at translating the New Testament into one of the 22 dialects of the Mixtec language. Although Tom, who was associated with the Wycliffe Foundation in Mexico City, held significantly more conservative theological views than the two campus ministers, a bond was established – and in the context of this bond, Tom expressed his need for financial and work team assistance in improving the lives of the villagers in Santa Cruz Mixtepec. From these initial conversations grew a United Methodist – Presbyterian mission effort, funded initially by *Operation Mixtec I* with a grant of $42,150 awarded by the Hunger Committee of the Board of Higher Education and Ministry of the

THE SHINING OF LIGHT: A HISTORY OF THE WESLEY FOUNDATION
AT THE UNIVERSITY OF TENNESSEE, 1922-2007

United Methodist Church, from funds made possible by the Conference of United Methodist Military Chaplains. Each campus ministry took separate work teams (with 14-17 persons per team) to Santa Cruz Mixtepec for two summers. The grant was later renewed by *Operation Mixtec II,* a grant of $27,252. The two combined grants made seven work teams possible during 1978-1982.

In order to evaluate the possibilities of the mission and to prepare for the writing of the grant proposal, Bob Parrott and John Wright traveled to southern Mexico in July 1977, flying into the village of Santa Cruz Mixtepec, 150 miles from Mitla, a suburb of Oaxaca, by a private Missionary Aviation Fellowship plane. The village was perched at an altitude of 4000 feet, making it necessary for the three-seater plane to land precariously on a sloping, improvised mountain runway. The Missionary Aviation pilot delivered Bob and John to the rugged mountainside, met there by Tom Ibach, and returned three days later to fly them back to Mitla.

The village was a wooded settlement of approximately 250 Mixtecs centered by an ancient wooden footbridge crossing a mountain stream. The concrete-block clinic was located on the village's main street. Two miles down the mountainside was a trading village, San Juan Mixtepec, where villagers went on Fridays for market day; two hours further down the mountain was the provincial town of Tlaxiaco. Although in the village there remained an empty, decaying church structure built and later abandoned by Franciscan missionaries in the late seventeenth century, the religious system embraced by the villagers was a form of animism embroidered with a few vestiges of Spanish Roman Catholicism. Although the people in Santa Cruz Mixtepec used Spanish money and had Spanish names, they were a native Indian-Mexican people who spoke only their own limited dialect. They were in critical need of help in learning (or re-learning) productive agricultural techniques (to augment their corn and beans diet) and the art of terracing land. They also needed assistance with basic hygiene practices and with improving the clinic building. They were desperate for help in bettering the grim condition of their lives, in which 35% of their children died before the age of seven, victims of worms, dysentery, whooping cough and measles.

Once Bob Parrott's written proposal was accepted by the Board of Higher Education and Ministry, extensive planning began. In March 1978, a team of five University faculty, including Dr. Neal Peacock, flew with Tom Ibach to the village site, where they planned the work. Throughout the project, Dr. Peacock's counsel was crucial. The mission operated on The Peacock Principle, "Do Not Go Down and Do Things For People Without Involving the People In the Process."

The Wesley Foundation team was the first to arrive in Santa Cruz Mixtepec (June 29-July 14, 1978) after traveling five days on the road in the old Foundation VW Microbus and in a rented Ford Club Wagon from Knoxville, and going the last few miles from Tlaxiaco up the mountainside on a precarious road by cattle truck. They slept on the floor in the empty rooms of a concrete-block schoolhouse; they bathed in the mountain stream, and ate their meals in the home of the Ibachs, where the primitive plumbing system allowed the toilet to be flushed only once a day. Tom's wife Neelie prepared meals for the group. Working under Tom's direction, and learning from him of the Mixtec culture, they planted cherry tomatoes and chickpeas, re-terraced ancient fields, and began a renovation of the clinic building. (They tried planting squash within the corn rows, but found that the villagers would not eat squash, considering it "pig food.") They also worked with Samuel Lopez Santiago, a young villager in his late twenties, who was the only baptized Mixtec Christian in the community. In order to greet villagers, they learned a few words of Mixtec, especially *'nixi nani ni'* (what is your name?) and *'tatsavini'* (thank you). Throughout the entire project, students were profoundly moved by the dedication and the work ethic of Tom Ibach. They celebrated worship in the bare schoolhouse every evening. They did not "preach" to the Santa Cruz Mixtepec people, but in spite of the language barrier, they were able to reach out in an incarnational mode to the villagers with friendliness and hard work. Their experience was *remarkable,* a venture in the conjunction of affluent North American values and a precarious Third World existence, a journey into the heart of evangelism. It was a life-changing week.

One of the most critical experiences of those who worked in the clinic renovation project was the death of a woman patient who had walked two hours from a neighboring village for medical care, and had been provided bed space for the night. When it was discovered that she had died during the night, students helped Tom Ibach and Samuel Santiago wrap the body in a sheet and place it outside in the street; messages were sent to her village that her relatives were to come to Santa Cruz Mixtepec and retrieve the body. In the fragile mountain world, death was a constant reality.

In contrast to the primitive life in the village, the work team spent a couple of days in Mexico City during the return trip, staying at a small hotel in the Zona Rosa. By the time they arrived at the Casa Hernandez, they were tired and grimy, but they had become – in different ways – different people. Members of the first Wesley Foundation work team were Edward Tucker, Steve Johnston, Alan McNabb, Earl Sheridan, Sally Zimmerman, John Allen, Sharon Rice, Kay Ray, Bobbie Newman, Julie Patterson, David Crownover, Bryan Jackson and Bob Parrott.

The deepest meaning of the 1978 summer mission is best described in summary reports written by these first team members. Eddie Tucker wrote, "My biggest worry about the entire trip was what impression we would make on the people of Santa Cruz Mixtepec. Our North American values differ so much from theirs;

STARS OVER SANTA CRUZ MIXTEPEC
(1977-1982)

there would be so much they did not understand about us and we could only try to understand them. Would the Mixtecs have a better understanding of what Christians are like by having our work crew in their village? This was perhaps the greatest opportunity I have had as a Christian to demonstrate as fully as possible the Christian way of life without preaching words. Enduring hardships, giving and expecting nothing in return, forgiving and loving could all be demonstrated simply with our actions." Steve Johnston said, ".....I spent my week in the village as a combination carpenter-electrician. Putting in a hung ceiling and fluorescent lighting in the clinic was right up my alley. I guess working there all week while Tom and Sam waited on patients gave me one of the closest views of the Mixtec people possible.....I know education can mean cultural change, but to see people living under conditions slightly higher than their livestock has to say something." Alan McNabb concluded, "Operation Mixtec is just another humanitarian project until one looks at a few simple facts, and then it becomes a Christian project. Funded by Christian organizations, the project is conducted under the leadership of a Christian missionary. Perhaps most important, the project is conducted with the idea of sharing a kind of care and appreciation which is nurtured in the Christian church. There are ample reasons to call Operation Mixtec a Christian Mission."

Sally Zimmerman quoted from her daily journal. "What does my work in the village say to the people?.....We went to show them how to build rock terraces, a cactus terrace, and a ceiling for the clinic. By building them, we demonstrated the value of caring for others.....I have been aware of the largeness of the world and the many different cultures through educational courses and listening to friends who have traveled, but it was different for me to actually see the world from a different viewpoint.....There is so much more to the world and all the people than I ever imagined....." Earl Sheridan said, ".....Although we did not go in preaching 'fire and brimstone,' I feel that our work was evangelical.....To me evangelism means spreading the Gospel. Usually this is done through preaching, but Christ's Gospel can also be spread through action. I feel we spoke through our actions....." John Allen reflected, "Although we came from worlds apart, there was a definite interpersonal force that enabled us to communicate with the villagers. The words of the Mixtec language we learned were superficial, but even this fact demonstrated a willingness to communicate, and the villagers responded very well. Sometime I think that cooperation was the ultimate form of communication....All of us are God's children, and we are to help one another." Sharon Rice said, "Going to Santa Cruz Mixtepec was like a journey through a time portal into the primeval past. My communication skills had been left behind in the space age of America.....I found that I could express my feelings toward a villager with a warm handshake that would say, 'I care about you and I'm really glad to be here.' I remember how wonderful it felt to grin at a villager and receive a nod of recognition....."

Kay Ray wrote, ".....The heart of the problem in Santa Cruz Mixtepec lies deeply in the lack of knowledge and deterioration of previous skills and knowledge. The civilization may yet survive if a system of teaching food production techniques, practical hygiene and nutrition can be developed. The serious erosion, animal control (wild dogs) and finding clean drinking water sources are problems that must be solved....." Bobbie Newman said, ".....The heart of the problem in Santa Cruz Mixtepec is an almost pre-Colombian culture struggling to survive in the 20th century while maintaining its unique identity....." Julie Patterson added her own theological perspective, ".....This mission is a Christian one because we recognize God as the source of help for the Mixtec Indians. We act only as His agents. The people owe us no debt; we expect no reward. The thanks belongs to God. This work isn't evangelical in the strict sense, but I think the effect on the people will be stronger than if we just came down and preached to them. Our low-key evangelism makes an impact by showing

STARS OVER SANTA CRUZ MIXTEPEC
(1977-1982)

people what Christ meant for them, not just telling them....." David Crownover, a senior anthropology student, wrote, "My perception of the world has changed. It now includes a greater awareness of the nearness and complexity of poverty. I do not take such things as possessions, ice and food for granted any longer. I feel myself re-evaluating my priorities and what is important to me. I feel more 'driven' to do something."

Bryan Jackson concluded, ".....While we hoped to introduce protein-rich foods such as chickpeas, eggs and milk into the diet, the more significant point is that we have attempted to improve the quality of life in Santa Cruz Mixtepec by respecting the cultural heritage of the Mixtec people and by working within the framework of this heritage rather than by attempting to alter it to match our middle-class North American values.....An interesting part of this experience was the opportunity to compare the way we approach our existence to the manner in which the Mixtec people approach theirs. In our world, we live for the challenge and excitement that the next day of an ever-changing society brings. The Mixtec seems to eke out a day-by-day existence with little thought of what tomorrow will bring. Imprisoned in a devolved and static society, the Mixtec seems to accept his fate, and seems resigned to a future with little hope of progress....."

The second year's work team (June 21-July 5, 1979) consisted of Eddie Tucker, Randy Corlew, Connie Finger, Sharon Rice, Sally Wright, Paul Wright, Linda Shuff, Robert Guinn, Kleide Alves, Mark Legan, John Mefford, Kirk Laman, Bryan Jackson and Bob Parrott.

By the second year, because of the rigors and dangers of ten days on the road, Bob Parrott raised extra money in order that the team could fly to Mexico City and then proceed to the small regional capital of Tlaxiaco by Mexican bus. The bus journey itself

> **MIXTEC Team in Mexico**
>
> OPERATION MIXTEC, the World Hunger project sponsored by the Wesley Foundation at the University of Tennessee, Knoxville (in cooperation with the Presbyterian Campus Ministry), begins its second summer with a work team of 14 persons who are currently in Cruz Mixtepec, in the Oaxaca Province of Mexico.
>
> Among the projects scheduled for this summer are the digging of a well and the installation of a water system for the existing Mixtec Clinic; an agricultural project, in which chickpeas and tomatoes will be introduced into the planting schedule; a nutrition and health project; and the digging of two community latrines.
>
> A second team, composed of students from the Presbyterian Center, left Knoxville on July 26.
>
> Operation Mixtec team members, from left, front row: John Mefford, Eddie Tucker, Kirk Laman, Mark Legan, Bryan Jackson; second row: Bob Parrott, Kleide Alves, Linda Shuff, Bob Guinn, Sharon Rice, Connie Finger, Randy Corlew, Paul Wright, Sally Wright.

Stars Over Santa Cruz Mixtepec, 1977-1982

was a study in contrasts, the UTK group carrying foodstuffs and building materials purchased in Mexico City, crowded together with Spanish-Indian passengers carrying chickens. They were met (as in 1978) by Tom Ibach with a cattle truck for the last section of the trip to Santa Cruz Mixtepec. (The Presbyterian team left Knoxville on July 26.) The work of the Foundation's 1979 team consisted of digging a well and the installation of a water system for the clinic, the construction of a "holding tank" platform for a future village water system, an agricultural project, the vaccination of village dogs (during which Mark Legan was bitten by an angry dog!), a nutrition and health project, and the digging of two community latrines.

Digging a latrine, 1979

In her summary report of the 1979 work, Connie Finger wrote, "The future for Santa Cruz Mixtepec is closing in. The land is wearing out, the Mexican government is pushing for the dissolution of culturally different groups, and the children are being educated in a different language. The future calls for change. I hope and believe that our visits may help prepare them for what is in their future….." Linda Shuff concluded, "Although Santa Cruz Mixtepec is sheltered from the outside world, it seems that their future will be dependent on change that will occur as a result of influence from the outside. Change seems unavoidable in their situation, and signs of outside influence can be seen in the rise of alcoholism and venereal disease among the villagers." Mark Legan wrote, "On the first day, three of our team accompanied by Sam and the village mayor we went on a surveying mission to scout out possible sources of fresh water. We investigated three springs that morning…..By the time we had walked about a mile, I was feeling sick.....From the morning's work we were able to determine a spring which might be a possibility for fresh water in the community.....By the end of the first day I had a miserable case of diarrhea which stayed with me until we were two days out of the village. Some of the others also came down with intestinal problems during the course of our stay. For those of us who contracted this problem the experience of being sick helped us to understand the kind of chronic problems the villagers have to deal with. Because of their constant exposure to bad water, many people in Santa Cruz live with constant diarrhea....." Today, Dr. Mark Legan is a practicing physician in Dyersburg, Tennessee.

A highlight of the second year's visit was a party planned for the children of the village. Working with Paula, a woman in the village who spoke Spanish and Mixtec, Kleide Alves – fluent in Spanish, Portuguese and English -- coordinated the activities. The party had been advertised on the village loudspeaker, and 70 children attended. Stories were told, songs were sung, art work was created, games were organized, and refreshments (carrots, tomatoes, lemonade and cake) were served. Before eating, each child was shown how to wash his or her hands, during which individual Polaroid photographs were taken. For some of the children, it was the first time they had ever seen a photograph of themselves. On days following the organized party, large numbers of children appeared every afternoon for more parties – and the merriment, food, and washing of hands continued. In addition, students constructed booklets in Mixtec (edited by Paula and Tom Ibach), entitled *?Nchi Tsini Nuhu Saha Cuee Mee Ta Nchaan Gaa Catsi Cuee Mee Cuee Chuhi,* meaning "How To Prevent Diarrhea," illustrating (with drawings) the art of washing hands and describing the choice of healthy food. The booklet was brought back to Knoxville, printed in 200 copies, and was mailed to Santa Cruz Mixtepec.

STARS OVER SANTA CRUZ MIXTEPEC
(1977-1982)

The village fiesta, 1979

The third Wesley Foundation work team (June 23-July 5, 1980) constructed an elegant two-hole village privy, conducted a Village Fiesta and nutrition project, dug a family well, planted different varieties of beans and peas, inventoried the facilities of the clinic, and provided funds for the construction of a Conasupo. Team members were Robert Stammer, Earl Sheridan, Jon Sayers, Jay Kaiser, Douglas Livesey, Mary Ellen Beckner, Diana Shrader, Sally Wright, Randy Corlew and Bob Parrott. By the time this team's work had been completed, a clear future plan had emerged – the building of a water system whereby a mountain spring one mile above the village could be tapped and spring water brought down the mountainside by p.v.c. pipe to holding tanks near the clinic, providing clean water for the entire village. Although Operation Mixtec had begun as a primarily agricultural project, the team realized that the need for good water was the crucial factor in Santa Cruz Mixtepec.

One of the most incandescent experiences during the work teams' visits in 1978, 1979 and 1980 happened in the evenings, after the evening meal and worship. Because the Mixtecs strongly objected to anyone walking in the village or on surrounding mountain trails after dark, the work teams remained closely at the schoolhouse and relaxed on the school's concrete playground, studying the vast constellations of stars moving across the equatorial sky, sights they had never seen before on such a cosmic scale. The darkness was so dark and the altitude so high and the southern vista so wide that they were experiencing an acute awareness of the heavens as if for the first time. Whole galaxies moved like armies across the summer night. They encountered rare, nightly shinings of light.

In summer 1981, an evaluation team – comprised of Doug Livesey, Jay Kaiser, Mary Ellen Beckner, Randy Corlew and Bob Parrott – traveled to Santa Cruz Mixtepec. There, they and Tom Ibach consulted with the village elders, participated in a village meeting of the townspeople, and located the exact site for tapping the mountain spring for the proposed water system. At the village meeting, one elderly man, speaking in Mixtec (as translated by Tom Ibach) attested to the changes that had occurred since 1978, principally the fact that not as many of the village children were dying. Their ancient custom had been to ring the old bell in the abandoned church building when a child died – now, he said, *'the bell doesn't ring as much.'*

The final phase of the entire Operation Mixtec project was completed during July 1982, when five Wesley Foundation engineering students – Jay Kaiser, Mike Fletcher, Randy Corlew, Doug Livesey and Edward Hancock – traveled to Santa Cruz Mixtepec, where they contrived, engineered and completed the water system, snaking the pipe down the mountainside to holding tanks on the village street. For the first time since the Mixtecs had occupied the site centuries earlier, villagers had a supply of fresh, clean water for drinking, cooking and washing.

STARS OVER SANTA CRUZ MIXTEPEC
(1977-1982)

69,262 miles were traveled during 1977-1972. Of this total, Wesley Foundation students traveled 53,740 miles. A total of 86 persons participated in on-site work projects; of this total, 46 were from the Wesley Foundation. Several people participated more than one time. By the beginning of the University's fall term in 1982, by means of the influence of work team members on the entire campus ministry, the Wesley Foundation was a changed, matured community.

An unexpected future lay ahead of Santa Cruz Mixtepec. The Mexican earthquake of 1983 which severely damaged Mexico City and other locations also caused havoc in the Mixtec village. The water system so carefully and joyfully constructed was totally destroyed – the concrete holding tanks and the mile of p.v.c. pipe lay in ruins. Tom Ibach died a few years later. Hopefully Samuel Lopez Santiago is still there, maintaining the clinic. The equatorial stars still shine!

2

Concurrent with the development of Operation Mixtec in Santa Cruz Mixtepec, the daily-weekly-monthly-yearly ministry of the Wesley Foundation in Knoxville continued.

Active leadership during the years 1977-1979 was offered by Kevin Crow, Melinda Sutton, Jay Parkins, Libby Bailey, Laura Langley, Karen Kiel, Meredith Montgomery, Bud Gilbert, Steve Johnson, Mary Miller, Deusdedit 'Dete' Furlan (a Brazilian student), and Bill Ledbetter. Earl Sheridan was Coordinating Cabinet president in 1977-1978. In spring 1978, new aluminum letters were mounted on the façade of the building, proudly declaring *Wesley Foundation, University Methodist Center,* an expression of the campus ministry's theology – the building was not exclusively a "student center" but was a "university center." The ministry was aimed at the entire university community.

THE SHINING OF LIGHT: A HISTORY OF THE WESLEY FOUNDATION AT THE UNIVERSITY OF TENNESSEE, 1922-2007

With little advance notice, the Lutheran Campus Ministries decided to relocate to other quarters. As a result, another serious financial dilemma for the Wesley Foundation was created. It became necessary to cut funds from program development, and immediately the Coordinating Cabinet organized fund-raising projects to address part of the problem. An emergency request was made of the Holston Conference Council on Finance and Administration, and additional monies were provided. Board President James Crook, who had followed Frank M. (Bob) Bostick as Board president, guided the ministry through a difficult period.

During an informal evaluation of the ministry by the Holston Conference Board of Higher Education in 1978, students reflected on the value of the Wesley Foundation to them. Among the written responses was the following: "…it is a place where I and others are freely accepted as we are. We can engage in honest inquiry and discussion concerning theology and the Church. It is probably the single most valuable aspect of my undergraduate career." Also, "…..it was the primary vehicle for my decision to enter the ministry….." And, "…..My experience at the Wesley Foundation enabled me to make the crucial connection between my academic commitments and my involvement in personal concerns and in concerns for issues of social change in the society at large….." During the students' participation in this evaluation, the 1978-1979 Coordinating Cabinet was led by Oak Ridge student Alan McNabb.

In spring 1978 the first of a long line of theatrical productions was presented to the campus and to the community in the Wesley Foundation Theatre, known as "Spring productions." *Spoon River Anthology,* a play by Edgar Lee Masters, was directed by Al Dodson. Since casting was always open to campus participation, involvement in the plays and audience attendance at spring productions became a vital port of entry through which campus students and others were introduced to the campus

STARS OVER SANTA CRUZ MIXTEPEC
(1977-1982)

ministry, and the Wesley Foundation began to acquire a reputation as a locus for high quality theatre productions.

The head resident for the academic year 1979-1980 was Mark Legan. Other members of the residential student staff were Danna Carter, Randy Corlew, Kevin Crow, Deusdedit (Dete) Furlan, Kirk Laman, Cindy Jo Maynard, Earl Sheridan, Eddie Tucker, Douglas Woody, Martin Kirk, Douglas Woody and Mary Miller. The elected president of the Coordinating Cabinet was Eddie Tucker, who presided over a busy schedule of events and activities, among them Wednesday Vespers, the WHAM ministry, and Friday Fling (a fellowship evening). Mark Legan and Paul Wright led a Sunday Bible study. Sunday Worship continued as the lynchpin of the ministry, with attendance ranging from 85 to 175. (In a cycle of four quarters, approximately 1800 different people were involved.) A free Sunday Luncheon following worship was prepared by local United Methodist Women's groups in the Knoxville and Maryville Districts; 30-60 persons were generally served every Sunday. The participation of the United Methodist Women became a vital, productive link with supporting churches. A new Wesley Foundation singing group was led by Al Dodson. In many configurations, approximately 300-325 people used the building weekly. Bob Parrott offered a year-long theological seminar entitled "The Development of Christian Thought," with an attendance of 10-12 people. There were three retreats; the combined total number of people served was 80. A delegation attended the Tennessee United Methodist Student Movement Retreat, February 22-27 at Tech-Aqua near Cookeville.

The rock musical, *Godspell,* directed by Cathy Hudson and Jim Frost (with musical direction and choreography by Tim Hinton and Jan Taylor), played to capacity crowds in the Theatre totaling 1,026 people for five nights, April 24-28, 1980. Playing Jesus was Eddie Tucker. Other cast members were Diane Bailes, Lisa Burgess, Debbie Burleson, Annette Cleveland, Chuck Comeaux,

Dan McCammon, Kellye McCrary, Kristy Parkins, Leslie Parrott, Wendy Pitts, and Earl Sheridan. The band was composed of Paul Wright, Bruce Warren, Bill Ledbetter, Tim Hinton and Steve Barton.

Godspell, **1980**

Through the Campus Ministers' Council, Bob Parrott's weekly evening assignment as "counselor and chaplain" at the University Apartment Resident Hall augmented his regular schedule of counseling appointments; he served with other campus ministers in regular visitation of students and faculty at University Hospital. As a resource person, he also began regular participation in classes on Human Sexuality in the College of Human Ecology. Preaching continued to be central to his understanding of the tasks of campus ministry, especially the effort to speak directly to the images and idioms then central to university young adults. In 1979, the sermon titles included "Who Owns the Earth?", "Violence,

STARS OVER SANTA CRUZ MIXTEPEC
(1977-1982)

Vanity and Cowardice: The Three Faces of All of Us (after reading *The Fall,* by Albert Camus)", "On Lust," "O Earth, You're Too Wonderful For Anybody To Realize You!", "Knowing Something, Even When You Don't Know It", and "Losing, Not Winning, Is the Name of the Game!"

By 1980, the excitement of the coming World's Fair in Knoxville (Expo '82) in the immediate neighborhood of the University began to heighten the intensity of the urban setting for the ministry.

Another serious financial crisis was experienced in 1980-1981, during which a special funds campaign was organized to raise monies to assist with the semi-annual mortgage payments. $4,232 was raised, which was applied to the building payment due December 31, 1980. At that time, the total amount of indebtedness remaining was $83,609. Special daily Lenten services began on Ash Wednesday and concluded on Good Friday; University president Jack Reese was one of the Lenten speakers. Attendance at Sunday Morning Worship increased – on some Sundays it was difficult to provide enough chairs, bulletins, and space. Often students sat in an extra rank of chairs placed on the Theatre stage. The high degree of congregational participation in worship may have contributed to the increase, coupled with a major return to campus group life and group identity on campus after the individualism of the late 1960s and early 1970s. A decidedly conservative theological shift in student attitudes and values was becoming apparent.

In mid-April 1981, in conjunction with the UTK Theatre Department, Gretchen Burleigh directed a production of *The Crucible,* by Arthur Miller, in the Wesley Foundation Theatre. It played to approximately 650 people. In the cast were John Beasley, Nancy Woody, Brenda Brown, Laura Lynn Griffin, Margaret

THE SHINING OF LIGHT: A HISTORY OF THE WESLEY FOUNDATION AT THE UNIVERSITY OF TENNESSEE, 1922-2007

Cooter, Scott Douglas, Katye Ross, Libby Bailey, Eric Eubanks, Wendy Pitts, John Cherry, Keith Cornelius, Tim Myatt, Dan McCammon, Katye Ross, Mike Bagwell, Al Dodson and Lorri Crump. Serving as properties/running crew were Ron Hughes and Bobby Burke. Handling publicity were Kevin Crow, Steve Frazier, Danna Carter and Eddie Tucker.

Jon Keith Sayers was the head resident in 1980-1981. The residential community included Jenny Andrews, Danna Carter, Scott Douglas, Martin Kirk, Wendy Pitts, Eddie Tucker, Trevor Cook, Mark Dinsmore, Daniel Roberts, Earl Sheridan, Douglas Woody and Deusdedit Furlan. Edward Tucker continued to head the Coordinating Cabinet for a second year.

The 1980 Annual Report to the Holston Conference reported the effect of the ongoing project in Santa Cruz Mixtepec on the year's ministry. "The Wesley Foundation's outreach is not parochial or denominationally exclusive – the ministry reaches many non-Methodists. The headquarters for this ministry is a comfortable and adequate building, but the mission reaches far beyond its confines, especially in the World Hunger emphasis in Mexico.....In a volatile campus setting of 27,000 people, this ministry still struggles to personalize the size and scope of the university community, offering a caring, redeeming, accepting Word."

During the academic year 1981-1982, at the end of which occurred the final trip to Santa Cruz Mixtepec, a Wednesday night discussion form, Kaleidoscope, was developed, and soon became a lively, well-publicized event. Offering opposing views on contemporary subjects drew sizeable crowds. Topics such as "Religious Cults and Charismatics" and "The Israeli-Palestinian Conflict" were covered by reporters from *The Daily Beacon.* The potentially unruly crowd present to hear the conflicting Israeli and Palestinian points of view necessitated the presence of University

STARS OVER SANTA CRUZ MIXTEPEC
(1977-1982)

security personnel. The regular program of weekly events continued, as did the increase in attendance at Sunday Morning Worship. On November 21, 1981, six UTK students were baptized and received into membership in the United Methodist Church; on May 30, 1982, two additional students were baptized and received into membership.

A musical revue, *Seasons: A Celebration of Life,* written by students Mike Bagwell, Tim Hinton and Gregory Sterchi, and involving 35 Wesley Foundationers, was presented on May 13-16, 1982. In the cast were Melissa (Missy) Adams, Belinda Burleson, Darlene Cash, Rob Cox, Bryan Decker, Tracy Doty, Jeff Ellison, Ellen Everett, Leslie Ferguson, Thomas Givens, Michelle Godfrey, Karol Hagen, Cindy Hatchett, Jay Kaiser, Martin Kirk, Doug Livesey, Dan McCammon, Angela Parks, Leslie Parrott, Wendy Pitts, Randy Schultz, Candace Jo Smith, Gregory Sterchi, MeLinda Tatum, Audrey Thompson, Eddie Tucker and Nancy Woody. Stage manager was Anne Lambrecht. Narrators were Ellen Everett and Mike Bagwell.

Seasons: A Celebration of Life, **1982**

THE SHINING OF LIGHT: A HISTORY OF THE WESLEY FOUNDATION
AT THE UNIVERSITY OF TENNESSEE, 1922-2007

In 1981-1982, Gregory (Greg) Sterchi was the head resident; the Community Fellows were Dan Roberts, Mike Bagwell, Deborah Burleson, Dan McCammon, Wendy Pitts, Katye Ross, Douglas Woody, Lorri Crump, Gary Harmon, Kris Hyberger and MeLinda Tatum. Douglas Woody served as president of the Coordinating Cabinet.

The attempt to articulate the purpose of the Wesley Foundation continued. The campus minister's Annual Report submitted in January 1982 commented, "The ministry strives to serve not only students but faculty and staff of the University, and intends to be not only a 'student ministry' but a 'campus ministry.' The visibility and availability of a university center like the Wesley Foundation affirms a basic theological presupposition, that the role of the Church is to care for persons with a clear redemptive Word and act wherever persons coexist and work with a structuring of ministry to meet the specific needs of a community. We struggle at working in the midst of a university community of knowledge and research and inquiry....."

Chapter IX

GO FORTH BELIEVING
(1982-1993)

1

An enlarged ministry with rising expenses and a stripped-down budget further complicated the Wesley Foundation's struggle to pay the semi-annual building payments of $6250, and created an urgent need to erase the building debt entirely as soon as possible. In early 1982, the Board of Directors, under the leadership of James Crook, waged another special funds campaign, this time seeking $12,500, in order that the doubled amount of $25,000 might be applied to reducing the debt. The campaign raised an extra $12,090, which was applied to the payment. By the end of December 1982, the amount owed on the building was $44,000.

During the academic year 1982-1983, Sunday Morning Worship continued to record large numbers of students attending – in fall 1981, there was a record congregation of 193. In fall 1983, the record was 186. By the early 1980s, there was an increase in the number of African-American and international students attending. Slowly, the experimental forms of worship and inventive congregational participation began to interest non-churched students for whom the Wesley Foundation was their first genuine experience of "church."

In 1982-1983, Charles R. (Randy) Corlew became president of the Board of Directors, the first Wesley Foundation alumnus to be named to this position. The 1983 Annual Report noted that the levels of programmed activity resembled a "three-ring circus, within which we attempt to design events/ activities/programming for varying sets of persons at different times for different reasons, in different forms -- offering different ports of entry." The spring production of 1983 was *Close Ties,* a play by Elizabeth Diggs, and directed by Mark Hipps, concerning a contemporary family's dealing with the issues of care for the elderly, sex, marriage, and the "generation gap." In the cast were Ruth A. Schneck, Jay Kaiser, Cindy Hatchett, Belinda Burleson, Angela Parks, Melissa Ritz, Randy Schultz and Ron Hughes. Michael Bender was the 1982-1983 president of the Coordinating Cabinet. Student leadership roles were filled by Deane Young, Jay Kaiser, Gary Harmon, Ellen Watson, Lorri Crump, Douglas Livesey, Mark Hipps and Thomas Givens. Residents were Jay Kaiser, Barry Shelton, Dan McCammon, Tracy Doty, MeLinda Tatum and Deane Young. Beginning work in September 1982 as the first female head resident was Cathy Joyce Crosby, a graduate audiology student, who continued in this post until May 1984. With quiet authority, Cathy was profoundly influential on many students. Today, she and her husband serve as teaching missionaries in The Ivory Coast in West Africa.

Jay Kaiser was the elected president of the Coordinating Cabinet for 1983-1984, his role now more clearly defined by his leadership in Operation Mixtec. Special activities for the year included an alumni Gala, a Christmas dinner prepared by Ada Jones, Kaleidoscope events presenting (on alternate nights) issues raised by Democratic and Republican candidates for the presidency, as well as the film *Bonhoeffer.* Study materials for the spring retreat included Leslie Weatherhead's *The Will of God.* The 1984 spring production was the Broadway musical *Carnival,* directed by Charles M. Reese, with music directors Sheryl Lawrence and Lisa Hunt. Presented in the Theatre May 19-22, the play's cast included Krista Marine, Cindy Hatchett, Scott Treadway, John Cherry, Crit Parrott, Charles M. Reese, Jenny Tilghman, Jill Hendrickson, Becca Wallace, Adam Light, Richard

GO FORTH BELIEVING
(1982-1993)

Bates, Ellen Everett, Robin Higgins, Richard Bates and Jay Kaiser. Costuming was supervised by Joanna Bender and Elizabeth Herren.

Work with latch-key children at Wesley House Community House continued, and planning began for a two-year community project (*Project Together*) in Mechanicsville, a near-campus residential area, on behalf of the elderly poor, for which a grant proposal was written by Bob Parrott. In reports to the Board of Directors, the campus minister expressed concern about the rising Fundamentalist mentality about religious matters on campus. At the same time, however, he reported a growing, broad-based student interest in the Wesley Foundation and commended the high quality of Wesley Foundation student leadership. Residents in 1983-1984 were Richard Bates, Darlene Cash, Tracy Doty, Thomas Givens, Jay Kaiser, Sheryl Lawrence, Deane Young and Scott Stroud.

Dr. Robert E. Bodenheimer was the president of the Board during the academic year 1984-1985 – a year of special significance -- because the final payment on the building was made to Hamilton National Bank in Johnson City on December 31, 1984, marking the end of the lengthy struggle to meet payments begun in 1965. A service of "note-burning" was celebrated in Sunday Morning Worship in February 1985, with Deane Young, president of the Coordinating Cabinet, and Bob Parrott setting fire to a copy of the loan document. (Momentarily, the document blazed too vigorously, and threatened to set fire to the surroundings!) Beginning in 1985, the budget was joyfully adjusted to accommodate the end of the mortgage payments.

The first backpacking trip to the Maroon Bells Snowmass Wilderness in the Colorado Rockies, led by Dr. George Everett, was made September 1-10, 1984.

THE SHINING OF LIGHT: A HISTORY OF THE WESLEY FOUNDATION
AT THE UNIVERSITY OF TENNESSEE, 1922-2007

Among active students in leadership roles in 1984 were Lisa Hunt, Sheryl Lawrence, Mel Stripling, Robert (Rob) Cox, Robert Haste, Mark Loy, Jenny Patton, John Sluder, Laura Stevenson, Doree Thompson, Jenny Tilghman, Dan Cragan, Ellen Everett and Laura Waltrip. Jay Kaiser served as head resident; the student staff included Richard Bates, Ellen Everett, Sheryl Lawrence, John Sluder, Doree Thompson, Mark Hipps, Patty Sargent and Sheung Shih-Chia. A second production of the folk opera, *Godspell,* with music and lyrics by Stephen Schwartz, was presented May 16-19, 1985; Scott McBride was the director, Sheryl Lawrence the music director and MeLinda Tatum the choreographer. A five-piece band featured Lisa Hunt, Avery Johnson, Sheryl Lawrence, Jim Wright and Paul Wright. Playing Jesus was Paul Ard III. Also in the cast were Wesley Allen, Shaun Brown, Fred Burriss, Mindy Chesney, Dan Cragan, Robin-Lynn Higgins, Michelle Oglesby, Audrey Thompson, and Susannah Zucker.

Following a trip to the Middle East with the American Friends Service Committee in April 1981, during which the team of clergy and educators interviewed PLO Chairman Yasser Arafat "across the Green Line" in Beirut, Bob Parrott became active in Friends of Palestine, a local Middle East group, to the displeasure of some of his Jewish and Christian friends. He also appeared on the *NBC Today Show* on November 5, 1984, objecting to anchorman Tom Brokaw's cavalier treatment of vice-presidential candidate Geraldine Ferraro during a nationally televised conversation.

In spring 1984, the Wesley Foundation received a grant of $8,952 from the United Methodist Church's Division of Higher Education for the development of Project Together, described as "a major service project in conjunction with Wesley House Community Center to work with the children and elderly poor of the Mechanicsville-Lonsdale-Beaumont areas of Knoxville." The

GO FORTH BELIEVING
(1982-1993)

plan focused on four major work weekends (October 26-28, 1984, February 22-24, 1985, April 12-14, 1985 and October 31-November 2, 1986) during which university students and senior high school students and community laypeople constituted "work forces" which ate, slept, and played at the Wesley Foundation, beginning with supper on Friday night, through a long Saturday work day, and concluding with worship and lunch on Sunday. Serving approximately 200 Mechanicsville residents in the Knoxville College area, the participants winterized homes, wrapped water pipes, raked leaves, cleaned gutters, did plumbing and electrical work, sawed wood, patched roofs, prepared gardens and constructed a playground unit. They painted houses, repaired roofs and rebuilt damaged chimneys. They experienced both cooperation and suspicion from some of the Mechanicsville residents on whose properties they worked. One experience long remembered by one work team was the day-long painting of a house, successfully completed while the residents of the house remained inside watching through the windows during the work. Students were surprised that the residents never emerged to express thankfulness for the day's labor. An important lesson was learned, that gifts given do not require gratitude.

KNOXVILLE, Tenn. — A work team of 43 persons completed PROJECT TOGETHER #5 Oct. 31-Nov. 2. The team worked on repair-renovation-restoration projects at nine locations in the Mechanicsville area of the city.
Sponsored by the UTK Wesley Foundation, the group of students staff, high school students, and laypeople from the Knoxville and Maryville districts are shown at Wesley House Community Center.

Project Together, **1986**

THE SHINING OF LIGHT: A HISTORY OF THE WESLEY FOUNDATION
AT THE UNIVERSITY OF TENNESSEE, 1922-2007

A memorable photograph of the October 31-November 2, 1986 work force weekend shows 31 people, including Wesley Foundationers David Rice, Sheung Chia, Jan Cabe, Lynwood Watts, Monica Taylor, Mike Howard, Sheryl Lawrence, Bob McNeil, Dan Cragan, and Mark Odom, plus high school students and community laypeople.

Following the completion of Project Together, a summary report, entitled "Getting It Together," detailed the work, its successes and failures. The report was distributed nationally by the United Methodist Board of Higher Education.

Deane Young and Kim Holden

GO FORTH BELIEVING
(1982-1993)

2

By 1985, partially in response to Operation Mixtec and Project Together, and in spite of its serious deficiencies, the Wesley Foundation in Knoxville was sometimes described (by bishops and others) as "one of the premiere Wesley Foundations in the Church." When the institutional question, "How many different persons has the UTK Wesley Foundation 'shared ministry' with during 1985?" was asked, the answer given by Dr. Robert E. Bodenheimer, Board president, and Bob Parrott was an astounding 6940, reflecting all the ports of entry opened – all the contacts, counseling sessions, the residential community, residence hall work, theatre productions, study courses, daily utilization of the building, UTK hospital ministry, marriages performed, Sunday Morning Worship, Cabinet activities, university classes, Project Together work, deputation teams and other opportunities for interpreting the campus ministry in local churches within the Holston Conference.

Laura Stevenson served as president of the Coordinating Cabinet for 1985-1986. In addition to Laura, student (residential) staff were Sheung Chia, Jenny Tilghmann, Doree Thompson, David Rice, Douglas Droppa, Laura Waldrip, Bonnie Rice, Sheryl Lawrence, and Robert McDaniel. Jay Kaiser continued as the head resident. Basic Bible, a continuing series of 1-hour mini-courses on Old and New Testaments, was offered by Bob Parrott. *You're a Good Man, Charlie Brown* was the Spring production, offered May 22-24, 1986, directed by Diane Crook, with musical direction by Lisa Hunt. The play, based on Charles Schultz' cartoon, "Peanuts," featured a four-piece band comprised of Bethany Bergan, Dan Duckworth, Lisa Hunt and Stephanie Ragsdale. The cast included Bill Hunt (Charlie Brown), Sheryl Lawrence (Lucy), Dan Cragan (Snoopy), Mark A. Williams (Linus), Jay Kaiser (Schroeder), and Laura Beasley (Patty). A review of the play in *The Daily Beacon* commented, "*Charlie Brown* may not have the spiritual thrust of a *Godspell,* but the decent humanity that Schultz's Peanuts celebrates is appropriate to the campus ministry's setting. Name a Peanuts' character and the results are a thousand character traits and idiosyncrasies that flood into your mind." A special Refurbishing Campaign in 1986 raised $4000, which provided a new sign for the front lawn, new draperies and carpet, and a newly upholstered sofa.

Rafting on the Nantahala

From its beginning, the Wesley Foundation had always been replete with abundant musical talent in the student community, forming various types of choirs, choruses, ensembles, and singing groups. The Wesley Foundation Chorale, subsequently named Cantabile, led by Sheryl Lawrence, a superb musician and composer, became well known on campus and in the three-District area for its artistry and professionalism. Cantabile became one of the chief interpreters of the Wesley Foundation's ministry to the local church constituency. Cantabile singers in the 1980s and early 1990s were Dawn Traynor, Doree Thompson, Stephanie Ragsdale,

GO FORTH BELIEVING
(1982-1993)

Lynne Dunn, Ellen Everett, Sheryl Lawrence, Laura Waldrip, David Rice, Jay Kaiser, Crit Parrott, Jamie Whoric, Eric Hartsfield, Everett Holmes, Mike Howard, Brian Inman, Chris McDaniel, Leslie Pitts, LaFreda Ball, Doug Bush, Kurt Haas, Kelly Payne, Van Pond, Jamie Thomas, Dana Truitt, Jonathan Waldrop, Laura Womack, Jia-Yue Yang, Steve Van Hooser, Barry Wallace, Mark Loy, Bill Hunt, Dan Cragan, Amie Allman, Sabine Barlow, Jim Bohy, Selina Duncan, Carol McNair, Jim Parks, Suzanne Shelton, Emily Abernathy, Jim Brogan, Kathy Dowlen, Shelley Hall, Rozella Harvey, Michael Hickerson, Marion Hurst, Susan Jones, Steve Key, Bob McLeary, Cheryl Mobley, Laura O'Kain, Todd Reynolds, Leslie Roberts, Travis Sharpe, Doug Shupe, Angela Snowden, Karen Wallwork, Barry Wallace. Lisa Hunt and Tao Lin were the major accompanists. During 1987, Cantabile sang before 2500 people, including 24 50-minute interpretive concerts in local churches and Holston Conference events.

There were serious, acknowledged weaknesses in the Wesley Foundation's campus ministry: an imperfect system of contacting students on campus, an imperfect system of assimilating students into the community, too few students involved in the actual day-by-day leadership of the Coordinating Cabinet, inadequate involvement in campus issues, and the need for constant enlargement and extension. Holston Conference officials sometimes complained that they were not getting "enough bang for the buck." Pressured by financial realities, the Board of Higher Education constantly reevaluated and re-studied the effectiveness of the campus ministry.

3

Charles (Chuck) McHose, a Holston Conference pastor, became president of the Board of Directors in 1986. A bright yellow brochure sent to all 2000 pre-enrolled students (who identified themselves as members of or interested in the United

THE SHINING OF LIGHT: A HISTORY OF THE WESLEY FOUNDATION AT THE UNIVERSITY OF TENNESSEE, 1922-2007

Methodist Church) at the beginning of the 1986-1987 year showed a smiling group of students in various poses gathered around the new Wesley Foundation sign on the front lawn at 1718 Melrose Place. Bill Hunt was the president of the Coordinating Cabinet, and was also a residential Fellow in a community which also included Jan Cabe, Monica Taylor, Bonnie Rice, Robert McDaniel, John Young, Dan Cragan, Lynne Dunn, Sheryl Lawrence, Mike Howard and Sheung Chia. Jay Kaiser completed his work as head resident in December 1986, followed by Lynwood Watts until August 1987. A new administrative secretary, Terri McBee, joined the staff, and became a valuable presence and a firm friend of students – she was often described as "the friendly face in the front office." The Board of Directors encouraged the development of a data base entitled "Friends of the Foundation," a large group of alumni, parents, former members of the Board, faculty, laypeople and others who could be identified as supporters and contributors to the life of the campus ministry. At the same time, the Board planned for the employment of a full-time Program Coordinator by fall 1988, and authorized a special funds campaign for this purpose.

After several months of work, a formal evaluation of the UTK Wesley Foundation mandated by the Holston Conference Board of Higher Education and Campus Ministry, was completed on January 18-29, 1987. A seven-person team led extensive interviews, consultations, and on-site visits. While the team identified strengths (in leadership, diverse participation, a capable staff, a balanced program emphasis, as well as a strong affirmation of the ministry by informed local churches), it also found significant weaknesses, termed "opportunities for growth" -- the need for more significant relationships with local churches, the need for an enlarged budget, more responsive seminars on campus areas of concern to students and faculty, and more thorough orientation of Board members. In its conclusion, the team reported, "This is a very active, interesting, and inspiring work. The Foundation is indeed the Church on the campus.....It is looked to for its creative programming and openness to those on the U.T. campus...This Foundation comes near to being a model Campus Ministry. It is a credit to the Church -- a creative, dynamic, influential witness to the UTK campus and to the world."

The Wesley Foundation received, in early 1987, a letter from Edward (Eddie) Tucker, by then an architect in Charleston, West Virginia, describing the effect of the campus ministry on his personal development. "Looking back on my time at UT and the Foundation, I remember some of the conclusions I drew about where and how I felt that I would be the best disciple for Christ. When I went to Mexico, especially my third year when I was there for 8 weeks, I realized that there was a great deal of mission work needed among the 'haves' as well as the 'have-nots.' Perhaps I was a better witness, I thought, to those who had much, and with it much responsibility for others less fortunate. And now, I find that at work, I'm surrounded by penultimate yuppies....I feel strongly that we will be held accountable someday as a wealthy nation and culture to how much we reached and sacrificed for others. I haven't done much, but I believe God is opening doors or presenting me with situations as if to say, 'O.K., you asked for your chance, so here it is!' I suppose I'm sharing this with you because the Foundation's ministry and witness did much to lead me, and I value that conviction and guidance and am thankful!"

In 1987, *Fiddler on the Roof,* based on the short stories of Sholem Aleichem, was the Spring production, directed by Sheryl Lawrence and Lisa Hunt, with choreography by MeLinda Tatum. *Fiddler* was played to an audience of almost 950, the largest in the long line of Spring production audiences. A significant number of the "Friends of the Foundation," including Bishop Kern Eutsler, the presiding bishop of the Holston Conferece, attended. Although it taxed the Foundation's resources and dominated everyday life during the time of its weeks of rehearsals, *Fiddler* set a new standard for spring productions as a crucial port of entry, through which many on-campus students (and others) were introduced to the Wesley Foundation's ministry. The cast included Ashley Ayres, Dan Cragan, Lynne Dunn, Ellen Everett, Nancy Harless, Eric Hartsfield, Mike Howard, Lisa Hunt, Mark Loy, Mark Odom, Crit Parrott, Leslie Pitts, Stephanie Ragsdale, Jill Rice, and Bob Parrott.

Dawn Traynor became president of the Coordinating Cabinet for the year 1987-1988, and serving with her in leadership roles were Mark Odom, Laurie Fagg, Chris Myrick, Douglas Bush, Eric Hartsfield, Jill Harris, Brian Inman, Lynne Dunn, Monica Taylor, and Dan Cragan. Sheryl Lawrence Howard was a staff assistant; Jan Cabe was a program assistant. Andrew (Andy) Lynch, a graduate student in sports physiology, became the head resident.

A new relationship with the campus African Student Association (composed of Christians, Muslims, and animists) began, and featured a holiday dinner given by the Wesley Foundation for 35 African students on December 27, 1987, many of them wearing the festive clothing of their respective countries. Active in the African Student Association was Kwame (Nana) Agyenim-Boateng, a Nigerian Ph.D. student, who soon became vital part of the Foundation's ministry, serving as president during 1988-1989 and as a member of the residential community.

Also in December 1987, five students and the campus minister attended Jubilee '87 in St. Louis, Missouri, a national student conference which (after more than 20 years) marked a resurgence of interest in a national network of United Methodist campus ministries. At the St. Louis Conference, Nana Agyenim-Boateng quickly established himself as a leader among hundreds of international students. Following Jubilee '87, there were regional student forums which finally urged the formation of a United Methodist Student Movement (UMSM) in 1993, which was made

GO FORTH BELIEVING
(1982-1993)

official by the 1996 General Conference of the United Methodist Church. Consciousness of the power and value of an organized student movement and student leadership, long dormant, had been resurrected.

The Spring theatre production of 1988 was the Hart-Kaufmann classic play, *You Can't Take It With You,* directed by Ashley Ayres. Included in the cast were Nancy Harless, Lisa Hunt, Theresa Gillard, Mike Howard, Phillip Smith, Michael Isbill, Matt Turner, Leslie Pitts, Chris Myrick, Mark Loy, Richard Bates, Lynne Dunn, Steve Louis, Ellen Myrick, Mark Odom and Randi Hunter. The stage managers were Karyn Repinski, Randi Hunter and Sheryl Howard; the scenic designer was Richard Bates; the master carpenter was Charles (Chuck) McHose.

One of the memorable experiences of the 1987-1988 academic year was a witness offered in Sunday Morning Worship during a sharing time (following the Word) when congregants stood and expressed joys, sorrows, concerns, and made requests for personal prayers. A Nigerian Ph.D. microbiology student, Oladele ('Dele) Olibia Ogunseitan – intelligent, handsome and very shy -- had been attending worship for several years, but had never shared joys or concerns. On this day, he stood and quietly announced that he had successfully defended his doctoral dissertation during the previous week, and would receive his doctorate at the summer commencement. When the applause subsided, he did not sit down. There was more. He said that he had accepted a post-doctoral fellowship at the University of California at Irvine, and after several years' absence, would finally be going home to Nigeria to see his family, probably by Christmas. There was more applause, but he still did not sit down. Then, hesitantly, he said, *"I want you to know that here in this place, in the Wesley Foundation on Sunday mornings -- for the first time in my life -- I have met Jesus."* There was silence. From some students such a statement might have seemed contrived, but not from 'Dele. From Oladele

THE SHINING OF LIGHT: A HISTORY OF THE WESLEY FOUNDATION
AT THE UNIVERSITY OF TENNESSEE, 1922-2007

Olibia Ogunseitan it was a genuine, heartfelt confession of faith. He continued, "....*Here in this place, I have met him, and I have identified him, and I have called him by his name, and now he goes with me when I leave.*" 'Dele sat down. Joys and concerns had been given new meaning.

The residential student staff in 1987-1988 included Sheung Chia, David Rice, Douglas Bush, Dan Cragan, Brian Inman, Monica Taylor, Eric Hartsfield, Bill Hunt, Jan Cabe, and Chris Myrick.

A new full-time Program Coordinator joined the staff in fall 1988, at the beginning of the new semester system instituted by the University. Pamela Rains, an ordained clergywoman in the American Baptist Church, assumed her position coordinating the regular, daily ministry activities at the Foundation, as well as working with further program development. As a result of her presence, the organization of the Coordinating Cabinet was further streamlined into four major work groups – Worship/Issues & Study, Service/Outreach, Foods/Fellowship, and Communications. Since 1988, a special funds campaign for the addition of the Program Coordinator had totaled $9401.

Members of the residential staff in 1988-1989 were Nana Agyenim-Boateng (who also was president of the Coordinating Cabinet), LaFreda Ball, Angel Edwards, Gina Gallagher, Brian Inman, Jerry Kennon, Richard (Rich) Irwin, Glenda Parrish, Michael Robertson, Susan Scheuring, Chris Slemp, and Jamie Whoric.

Two simultaneous DISCIPLE study groups, which had begun during the 1987-1988 academic year, were led by Bob Parrott. One group was comprised of students, and another was organized for faculty, church professionals and community laypeople. Each group formed met in a 34-week cycle for a

GO FORTH BELIEVING
(1982-1993)

minimum of 2 hours and 15 minutes. The campus minister's speaking schedule within the Holston Conference provided a further means of outreach, particularly on the topics "Cults," "The New Age Movement," and "Understanding Young Adults." He continued as editor of the weekly "Campus Ministers' Commentary" in the *Daily Beacon* (with a daily circulation of 18,000), in which CMC personnel addressed questions of religious, moral and global significance to the campus.

Pamela Rains, her husband Tim Rains, five students and Bob Parrott attended a UMSM Regional Conference in New Orleans in late December 1988. A highlight of the experience was dinner at Madame Tujaque's in the French Quarter.

The threats of world terrorism became more ominous with the December 1988 explosion of Pam Am flight 103 over Lockerbie, Scotland. A new age was suddenly real on the UTK campus, and many were alarmed. Writing in the Campus Ministers' Commentary in *The Daily Beacon,* Bob Parrott (trying to respond to the urgent question, 'Where was God when the plane went down?") wrote, "As a Christian, I know that God is powerfully and mysteriously with us, deep in our lives. God moves for good within whatever situations happen to us, regardless – not as a stage manager controlling our decisions, not as a grand puppeteer, not as the master of dancing marionettes – but as a loving Father, as a steadfast presence, willingly sharing in the consequences of creation......Whether the plane lands smoothly or is bombed over Lockerbie, whether life seems fair or not, whether we live or die, the God manifest in Jesus is always with us, giving us risky freedom, redeeming our brokenness....The most powerful sign I see comes not from a sudden last-minute change in the natural order where God swoops down and rescues us from danger, but in the continuing trust God teaches, where we love one another, where we struggle for justice, where we witness to the God who shares in every firestorm of our lives. This is the God who gathered those passengers and crew in his arms as they sped to earth. This is the God who never, never leaves us alone."

Another rousing musical revue, *Hooray for Hollywood,* written by Rosemary Ahmad, was the Spring production in 1989, directed by Ashley Ayres, presented April 21-22. . The music director was Lynne Dunn Bush; the choreographer was Audrey (Drey) Thompson; accompanists were Barry Wallace and Dawn Traynor. The play starred Drew Batchelor, Richard Bates, Dennis Bivins, Courtney Harris, Audrey (Drey) Thompson Herron, Nick Lanier, Christine Manikas and Jennifer Napier.

In April 1989, the strained budget (a perennial dilemma) did not permit Pamela Rains to continue in her position; continuing financial considerations prevented the hiring of another Program Coordinator. In fall 1989, Hughes Johnson began as a part-time staff assistant.

**Bill Hunt and the WHAM kids,
1989 Hallowe'en Party**

GO FORTH BELIEVING
(1982-1993)

The recognition and celebration of the parents of Sunday Morning Worship congregants began in spring 1989 with special Parents' Days, at which time red roses from the altar were presented by students to their attending families. Lunch for the congregation was served afterward. In preparation for the 1989 Parents' Day, a new benediction was written by Bob Parrott, and was sung congregationally to a traditional Spanish melody (#356 in *The United Methodist Hymnal*). A first verse was sung with accompaniment, followed by a second verse *a capella*. The congregation's harmonized singing of the benediction rapidly became the signature of the worshipping experience. It still continues.

> Go forth in goodness, for in Christ is goodness.
> Go forth in justice, it is of the Lord.
> When we are loving, when we are giving,
> We belong to God, we belong to God.
> (*a capella*)
> Go forth believing, go forth forgiving,
> Go forth in courage, in the hands of God.
> When we are loving, and are forgiving,
> We belong to God, we belong to God.
> We belong to God, we belong to God.

At the annual meeting of the Holston Conference at Lake Junaluska, North Carolina, in June 1989, a resolution of appreciation was presented to Bob Parrott for his "exceptional, extended tenure of appointment as the campus minister at the UTK Wesley Foundation." Recognizing that he had completed 25 years of "meritorious service" at UTK, the resolution declared that his leadership had "contributed immeasurably to a widely acclaimed model of campus ministry that has brought honor to the Holston Conference and fostered the on-going life of the Church." The resolution was also a clear affirmation of the 25 years of superior student and Board of Directors leadership based at 1718 Melrose Place.

4

Members of the residential community in 1989-1990 were LaFreda Ball, William DePriest, Garner Dewey, Valerie Ireson, Julia Morse, Joe Payne, Kelly Payne, Jan Albert Ringger, Todd Sutherland, Amy Wildman, Laura Womack, Marty Seals and Richard Irwin. Glenda Parrish served as head resident, beginning in June 1989. President of the Coordinating Cabinet was Richard Irwin. (Today Richard Irwin is an ordained United Methodist pastor in the Western North Carolina Conference.) Assuming key leadership roles were Van Pond, Jonathan Waldrip, Todd Sutherland, Nina Sharp, Mark Odom, William DePriest and Amy Wildman.

On April 5-8, 1990, the spring production was the classic favorite, *The Fantastiks,* with book and lyrics by Tom Jones and music by Harvey Schmidt. The director was Ashley Ayres; the musical director was Sheryl L. Howard, who was part of a four piece band also comprised of Drew Batchelor, Jay Miller and Ron Hubbard. The cast included Matthew Mitchel, Dan Cragan, Barry Wallace, Laura Beth Wells, Jason Garrett, Chip Hicks, J.L. Napier, and Richard Bates.

The ensemble Cantabile, under the direction of Dana Truitt in 1990-1991, continued as a major voice in interpreting the Wesley Foundation's ministry to area churches. Interpretation of the Wesley Foundation was made more strategic by the rightful demands for accountability of the support provided by Conference and District funds. Julia Morse was the elected president of the Coordinating Cabinet. Included in the student core leadership were Amie Allman, Joe Payne, Jim Bohy, Anna Brown, Wes Fanning, Salina Duncan, Todd Sutherland, Eric Hartsfield, Valerie Ireson,

GO FORTH BELIEVING
(1982-1993)

Matt Mitchel, Mark Odom, Marty Seals, and Kristi Shumaker. David Horsewood worked as a part-time staff assistant in fall 1990. Following his resignation in January 1991, Nancy Waller served in the position.

Outreach in the campus and Knoxville communities continued in 1990-1991 with four Saturday work days in Habitat for Humanity projects, weekly participation in WHAM with latch-key children, a Thanksgiving Dinner for international students, and dinner served at Dismas House, a transitional house for recently released prisoners in Knox County. The participation of Cantabile in the UTK All-Sing on February 2, 1991 brought excellent reviews and campus-wide attention. (The audition ratings for the Wesley Foundation ensemble were the highest on the campus, of 24 groups.) Two concurrent Community and student DISCIPLE groups continued. Thursday Luncheon was served to record crowds, the highest attendance of which was 155. Two students were financed to work in Nicaragua in May 1990 for Habitat for Humanity. During 1990, Sunday Morning Worship witnessed 4 baptisms, 9 baptismal renewals, and 3 members received into the United Methodist Church. A collection of faith stories, entitled *God Goes With Us,* representing the six Wesley Foundations in the Holston Conference, contained 4 UTK entries.

An Open House and dinner, in November 1991, celebrated the almost fifty years in which the Wesley Foundation had been established on campus -- since 1942 had marked the appointment of J. Irvin McDonough (Mr. Mack) as the first full-time campus minister and the beginning of planning for a separate Center building. The long succession of fifty years of Wesley Foundation student communities was the focus of the evening. Members of the Board of Directors and its president, Calvin Tipton, were present.

The Spring production of *Camelot* in 1991, directed by Barry Wallace, with musical direction by Dan Cragan, was at that time the most creative effort in the history of the Foundation's theatrical offerings. It played for seven consecutive nights, April 20-27. The players were Jonathan Waldrop (King Arthur), Dana Truitt (Guenevere), Gary Bynum (Lancelot), James Bohy, Roger Wallace, Laura Womack, Mark Odom, David Leach, Kevin Taylor, Leslie Roberts, Anna Brown, Michelle Rabensteine, and Bob Parrott (Merlin). Ladies of the Court were Selina Duncan, Shelley Hall, Suzanne Joy, Theta Wagner, Susan Winegar, and Laura Womack. Knights of the Round Table were Tom Reed, Barry Wallace, and Roger Wallace. The three piece band was comprised of George Hall, Dan Cragan and Matt Mitchel.

Camelot, 1991

Members of the 1990-1991 residential community were Rich Irwin, Matthew Mitchel, Joe Payne, Charles Pritchard, Marty Seals, James Bohy, Todd Sutherland, Dana Truitt and Cynthia Vesser. Glenda Parrish concluded her work as head resident in May 1991.

GO FORTH BELIEVING
(1982-1993)

Bob Parrott assumed a new pastoral relationship to the residents of Hess Hall, across the street from the Wesley Foundation. He worked directly with the residence hall director and the 14 RA staff members, and was available as a counselor at Hess Hall two evenings a week from 9:00 – 12:00 p.m. A large number of Hess Hall's custodial staff became regular attendees at Thursday Lunch; custodial personnel also became counselees. In addition, the Wesley Foundation gained one of its most valuable assets – Samuel Mason, who had retired as a custodian at Hess Hall, became the Foundation's custodian, jack-of-all trades and grandfatherly presence.

Mark Odom began work as head resident in June 1991. In September 1991, John Wadhams became the music coordinator and director of Cantabile. The residential community for 1991-1992 included Anna Brown, Shelley Hall, Eric Hartsfield, Pete Howard, Reed Humphrey, Robert (Bob) McLeary, Stephen Patek, Joe Pyle, Leslie Roberts, and Karen Wallwork. Theta Wagner was president of the Coordinating Cabinet. A strong cadre of student leadership included Anna Brown, Alan Cloar, Wes Fanning, Shelley Hall, Leslie Roberts, Joe Pyle, Susan Jones, Chris Knear, Latanya Daniel, Karen Wallwork and Simone McClellan.

The fall retreat at Camp Tri-Point, in October 1991, was an ecumenical event jointly with the Presbyterian campus ministry and John XIII Catholic Center. One of the memorable experiences of this week-end was a joint Eucharistic service combining the liturgies of the three churches. Other annual activities included the Holston Conference Student Retreat, a Fall Hayride and a Mardi Gras Frolic.

Another evaluation team, commissioned by the Holston Conference Board of Higher Education and Campus Ministry, completed several months of work by meeting at the Wesley Foundation September 6-7, 1991 for the purpose of evaluating the

THE SHINING OF LIGHT: A HISTORY OF THE WESLEY FOUNDATION
AT THE UNIVERSITY OF TENNESSEE, 1922-2007

UTK campus ministry's quality of performance, integrity of mission and response to the missional goals of the United Methodist Church. While again identifying strengths (in leadership, location of the building, high employee morale, diversity and balance of ministry, and an effective DISCIPLE program), the Team found obvious weaknesses – the United Methodist Women leadership in the Maryville District expressed strong feelings of being excluded from the Wesley Foundation's ministry; the 20% of self-generated income in the Board budget support needed to be expanded, and more emphasis was needed on alcohol–related campus problems. In general, the team reported "the distinct impression that this Wesley Foundation is an effective, active and vital ministry at UTK. It is truly a 'Church on Campus.' It has strong leadership and a very real sense of Mission....This Foundation is a credit to Christ and the Church."

5

Throughout the long history of the Wesley Foundation, beginning by the mid-1920s, a remarkable number of couples who were active in its ministry met (at the Foundation) and dated and became engaged and married. Others met elsewhere but dated and became engaged while either one or both were active Wesley Foundationers. Many of these recall the specific campus ministry event or occasion at which they became acquainted. Many were married either in the Chapel or in the Theatre; others were married in their home churches. All of them found that the Wesley Foundation was a supportive place in which to make life partner decisions.

The list of married couples is long. Among others, included among those who made marriage decisions in the setting of the Wesley Foundation during the years 1964-1993 are

    Arthur H. Miller - Margaret Anne Shanks
    Stephen E. Stout – Janie Daniel

GO FORTH BELIEVING
(1982-1993)

Thomas G. Parker – Wanda Shoemaker
David E. Walker – Donna Ann Blakely
Joseph D. Bishop – Dorothy Bangs
Donald Wayne Eskew – J'Lain Norris
Arthur Ellis – Charlotte Babcock
Lynn Sheeley III – Bonnie Frerichs
Charles B. Johnson – Mary Pennington Boyd
John Charles Waldrup – Margaret Ann Robinson
Joe Huber – Annie Laura (Susie) Thompson
David Torrance – Kris Hyberger
Robert W. Walton – Gwendolyn Harville
Randall Bass – JoAnn Fisher
Wade Lettsinger – Patty Preston
Robert Shirley – Janice Macy
Brian Moss – JoAnn Creger
Philip Pingchu Young – Nancy Jane Lundy
Stephen Campbell – Gayle Pierson
Stephen Johnston – Sandra Hundley
Thomas N. Jones – Kathryn Mitchell
Bryan A. Jackson – Elizabeth Widner
Lea Ousley – Linda Huddleston
Van Baxter – Diane Netherland
Paul Wright – Sally Zimmerman
Robert W. Patterson – May Kay Buchanan
Jeffrey French – Beverly Ann Simmons
Luther E. Galyon – Cynthia Daugherty
Clifton Marcev – Connie Ann Finger
David Crownover – Melinda Sutton
John Mark Legan – Mary Miller
Kirk Laman – Linda Lea Shuff
John W. Van Winkle – Carol Ketchersid
William Ledbetter – Deborah Sue Burleson
John Sluder – Darlene Cash
Danny Armstrong – Diana Shrader
Gregory Donoghue – Libby Bailey

THE SHINING OF LIGHT: A HISTORY OF THE WESLEY FOUNDATION
AT THE UNIVERSITY OF TENNESSEE, 1922-2007

John W. Young – Laura Ann Stevenson
Michael Howard – Sheryl Ann Lawrence
Michael Bender – Martha Susong
Ronald Hughes – Elizabeth Herren
Crit Parrott – Stephanie Anne Ragsdale
Jonathan Waldrop – Kelly Payne
Joe Payne – Nina Sharp
Christopher Myrick – Ellen Everett
Stephen Patek – Dana Truitt
Jay Alan Kaiser – MeLinda Tatum
Douglas Bush – Lynne M. Dunn
Kevin Crow – Leanna Cate
Brian Inman – Jan Cabe
Mark Loy – Valerie Ireson
Barry Wallace – Laura Womack
Todd Sutherland – Kristi Shumaker.

6

At a meeting of the Board's Executive Committee on October 17, 1991, Bob Parrott announced his intention to retire in June 1993, allowing the Board sufficient time to find a new campus minister. Having arrived at the Wesley Foundation in June 1964 at age 33, he would be leaving the post at age 62, a record for longevity of tenure in United Methodist campus ministry.

A new method of choosing student leadership for the Coordinating Cabinet, instituted in spring 1991, worked well. Instead of the usual voting procedure, students who desired to be considered for Cabinet offices posted a statement of their qualifications and leadership skills, and these persons were listed on the ballot. Voting was done by choosing from this panel. Consequently, the five top student leaders elected met together and chose one of their number as President of the Cabinet and the student community. The five students for 1992-1993 chosen were

GO FORTH BELIEVING
(1982-1993)

Theta Wagner, Alan Cloar, Kermit Parks, Michael Hickerson, and Cheryl Mobley. Theta Wagner was chosen President, and serving with her as co-president was Cheryl Mobley.

    The spring production in 1992 was the musical *Guys and Dolls,* "a musical fable of Broadway," directed by Barry Wallace, who had begun as staff assistant in summer 1991. Playing April 24-26 and May 1-3, the cast included Bob McLeary (Sky Masterson), Laura Womack (Sarah Brown), Roger Wallace (Nathan Detroit), Theta Wagner (Miss Adelaide), Todd Reynolds, Barry Wallace, Natalie Hatfield, Susan Winegar, Liz Waugh, Kellye Crowder, Tom Reed, Lindsay Bellas, Marian Baxter, Mike Musick, Cheryl Mobley, Angela Snowdon, Jonathan Waldrop, Shelley Hall, Fred Martin, Dan Cragan, Leah McRae, Emily Abernathy, Hope Alley, Judy Moore, and Reed Humphrey. The three-piece orchestra was formed by Susan Larson Frazier, Amie Allman and Laura McGinn.

***Guys and Dolls*, 1992**

THE SHINING OF LIGHT: A HISTORY OF THE WESLEY FOUNDATION AT THE UNIVERSITY OF TENNESSEE, 1922-2007

Alan Cloar and Cheryl Mobley led a mission team in spring 1992 to work at the Dulac Mission, an extension of the Sager Brown Institute of the United Methodist Church, on behalf of indigenous Louisiana Indians in Baldwin, LA. In the course of this trip, during which there was significant automotive difficulty with the rented van, they visited the Wesley Foundation at the University of Louisiana at Lafayette and also Vermillionville, the reconstructed Acadian village.

During the summer of 1992, after 25 years, the major compressor in the air-conditioning system in the building ceased all functioning. After years of patching and fixing, it was no longer repairable. Through the responsiveness of the resident bishop, Clay F. Lee, an anonymous gift of $12,000 was given to the Wesley Foundation toward the purchase of a new compressor, with the understanding that the Board of Directors would raise the additional funds needed to pay the balance on the bill. An additional amount of $5000 was raised by the Board of Directors, under the leadership of Calvin Tipton.

A quadrennial statement of mission, having been formulated by the Wesley Foundation and adopted four years earlier on April 12, 1988, was used to analyse the campus ministry's efforts and failures during the time period 1988-1992. The statement echoed the direction charted clearly as early as 1967 with the opening of the new building on Melrose Place. "The UTK Wesley Foundation is called to be and enact the United Methodist Church in the midst of the university campus; while maintaining a distinctive United Methodist identity, it is called to be an assertive ecumenical force as part of the Body of Christ.....Mission grows out of values and a living faith. The Wesley Foundation can minister effectively...only if it adheres to the power of Christian discipleship, the development of talent and opportunity, and a genuine care for persons." It was acknowledged that the effectiveness of the statement of mission would be rightly judged

GO FORTH BELIEVING
(1982-1993)

only in the future – by the faithfulness and discipleship of students and their influence in the wider world.

The search for a new campus minister, chaired by Darris Doyal, Knoxville District Superintendent, and involving Board members, faculty, students, and District laypeople, accelerated in 1992-1993. Mark Odom continued as the head resident. The community of residents included Alan Cloar, Aimee Allman, Bob McLeary, Joe Pyle, Michael Hickerson, Ruben Mamani, Alicia Felts, Cheryl Mobley, and Lori McNabb. The leadership cadre included Anna Brown, Andy Burgess, Judson Dunlap, Wes Fanning, Julia Morse, Leslie Roberts, and Travis Sharp.

A special service of recognition was held on March 10, 1993 in Nashville, at the office of the United Methodist Board of Higher Education and Ministry, Office of Loans and Scholarships, honoring Bob Parrott as campus minister and United Methodist Student Loan Representative, recognizing his 35 years of administering student loans (in three campus ministries, ULL, LSU and UTK), totaling approximately $2,000,000.

Inherit the Wind, subtitled *A Modern Courtroom Drama,* dramatizing the 1925 Scopes Trial in Dayton, Tennessee, was played in the Theatre on April 15-18, 1993. Barry Wallace was the director. The cast included Shelley Hall, Tyler Koontz, Susan Winegar, Michael Hickerson, Barry Wallace, Ruben Mamani, Alicia Felts, Andy Kneeland, Fred Martin, Ralph Boles, Kellye Crowder, Robin Thieme, Roger Wallace, Leslie Roberts, Chris Baldwin, Jonathan Waldrop, Anna Brown, Cheryl Mobley, Alexia Henke, Laura Wallace, and Charles Bailor.

Organized by an "Appreciation Task Force," a celebration was held on the weekend of April 24-25, 1993, marking the imminent retirement of Bob Parrott. A celebratory banquet was served at Church Street United Methodist Church, with Al

Yeomans as master of ceremonies and dinner music provided by Susan Frazier. There was a concert by Cantabile, under the direction of Bob McLeary, and four speakers were included in the evening's program – Lutheran campus minister Bill Couch, Dr. Wayne Cummings, and two alumni, Dr. Earl Sheridan and Dr. Kleide Alves. Scheduled to speak was Dr. Neal D. Peacock, who was unable to be present because of illness. Darris Doyal announced that Knoxville Mayor Victor Ashe had declared April 24, 1993 as "Rev. Robert Parrott Day." Special guests for the banquet were Bob's four grandchildren – 4-year old Ashley, and the 2-year-old triplets, Kristin, Alexander and Benjamin. On the next day, a special Sunday Morning Worship (with Bill Couch as preacher) was celebrated, followed by lunch in the Community Room. One of the features of the weekend was the announcement that the Wesley Foundation Theatre had been officially named the "Robert Parrott Theatre," now appropriately adorned with an engraved plaque.

On the last Sunday of June 1993, Bob Parrott completed 29 years of work at the Wesley Foundation. Following Sunday Morning Worship in the Theatre and lunch in the Community Room, he cleaned the kitchen, filled the coke machine, walked through the building a last time, sat in the Chapel for a few minutes, and left his bunch of keys on the campus minister's desk in the office. The years had been good.

Chapter X

A NEW DAY
(1993-2002)

1

Enoch L. Hendry, the fifth full-time campus minister of the UTK Wesley Foundation, was introduced to the Board of Directors on April 13, 1993. Articulate and energetic, Enoch had served (among other appointments) as the campus minister at the Clemson University Wesley Foundation, Aiken, South Carolina for six years, and arrived at UTK with strong qualifications and recommendations. He was an ordained elder in the South Georgia Conference of the United Methodist Church. At the Board meeting, he introduced his wife, Ann Curry, and his children, 4-year-old Phillip Walker and 15-month-old Coran James. Beginning work officially on July 1, 1993, he brought a fresh voice and new light to the Wesley Foundation.

At the April 13, 1993 Board meeting, Terri McBee, secretary-administrative assistant, was given a gift of $650 "in appreciation and confirmation" of her services and ministry. Terri continued as a valuable member of the staff, as did grandfatherly custodian Sam Mason.

Planning for the new academic year began immediately. A Spring Break mission trip (1994) was organized to the Texas-Mexico border region, in conjunction with the Presbyterian campus minister, Steve Musick, who had already established a working relationship with a PCUSA ministry, Puentos de Christo

THE SHINING OF LIGHT: A HISTORY OF THE WESLEY FOUNDATION
AT THE UNIVERSITY OF TENNESSEE, 1922-2007

(Bridges of Christ) in the McAllen, Texas region and across the Mexican border in Reynosa.

Cheryl Mobley chaired the Coordinating Cabinet in 1993-1994. Other students taking leadership roles were Andy Kneeland, John Sammons, Travis Hooper, Selina Duncan, Tripp Mullins, Carmel Skeen, Ruben Mamani-Paco, Susan Jones, Alicia Felts, and Susan Sowders. Alan J. Cloar became the head resident and staff assistant. The residential community included Michael Hickerson, Linda Lai Kwan Lam, Esther Lee, Ruben Mamani-Paco, Wintress Reynolds, Alan Smith, Sherri Smith, and Betty Mutwiri. Highlights of the academic year, in addition to DISCIPLE Bible Study, WHAM, Thursday Luncheon, work with Habitat For Humanity and Sunday Morning Worship, were a Fall Saturday Hike through Cades Cove to Abrams Falls in the Great Smoky Mountains Park, a Halloween carnival and a Christmas party for the children at the Wesley House Community Center.

At the Advent–Christmas candle lighting service in the Chapel on December 1, 1993, a special gift -- new green and purple altar paraments, given by Mrs. Evelyn McDonough, widow of J. Irvin McDonough – were presented to the Wesley Foundation. The gift was given in honor of Ruth DeFriese, who had been among the original promoters and supporters of the Wesley Foundation during the 1940s. The paraments also clearly commemorated the enormous imprint Mr. Mack had made on the beginnings of the Wesley Foundation's first years as it became established with a building on campus.

Planning for the Spring Break 1994 mission trip continued, involving a joint community of 20 Wesley Foundation-Presbyterian campus ministry students prepared to build houses and staff clinics in the USA-Mexico border area. However, it became necessary that Presbyterian participation (except for two students) was cancelled because the Musicks were expecting a

A NEW DAY
(1993-2002)

child in spring 1994, and Steve Musick was unable to make the trip. John Ardis, one of the Paulist campus ministers at John XXIII Catholic Center, agreed to provide eight students plus additional financial support for the project. The mission trip, as an ecumenical venture, was a resounding success. Included in the Wesley Foundation crew were Alan Cloar, Carmel Skeen, and Ruben Mamani-Paco. Two UTK nurses, who worked in the mission clinic, also accompanied the group. It was to be the first of seven mission trips made between 1994-2001.

**Wedding of Cheryl Mobley and Alan Cloar;
Enoch Hendry, officiating, 1994**

THE SHINING OF LIGHT: A HISTORY OF THE WESLEY FOUNDATION
AT THE UNIVERSITY OF TENNESSEE, 1922-2007

On April 14, 1994, concern was expressed to the Board of Directors by a Wesley Foundation alumna because of a speech which had been made (at the Foundation) by Chris Glaser, a gay activist and author of *Coming Out To God* and other books. The alumna requested that the Board define a structure which would determine the types of events which could be held at the Wesley Foundation, as well as who could or could not be allowed to speak. There was considerable discussion on the issue. Under the leadership of Board president Don Hill, no action to establish such a policy was taken and no such limitations were put in place.

In fall 1994, Andrew (Andy) L. Oliver, a junior seminary student at Candler School of Theology (Emory University, Atlanta, GA), joined the staff as seminary intern, program assistant and head resident, and continued through Fall 1995, at which time Edward (Eddie) Dorn assumed the leadership role. John Sammons served as president of the Coordinating Cabinet for the academic year 1994-1995. Other students involved in leadership roles were Kristi Jones, Eric Lopez, Carmel Skeen, Ruben Mamani-Paco, Rebecca Kerr, Jon Harris, and Travis Hooper. UTK students played a key role in compiling and distributing a newsletter for the Southeastern Jurisdiction Student Movement, created at Lake Junaluska, NC in October 1994. Travis Hooper wrote in the first newsletter, "The SEJSM was established for the benefit of all Methodist students and Wesley Foundations across the entire southeast. Wesley Foundations and students now have a voice and someone to turn to when no one will listen......the purpose of this paper is to form a network to relay programs that work, global connections, inspirational news, leadership training, prayers and devotionals and maybe even some fun."

As early as October 1994, planning for the Spring Break 1995 mission trip to the USA-Mexico border region was begun, a joint United Methodist-Presbyterian-Catholic project. The work force in 1995 was formed by a total of 38 participants. Of those, 32

A NEW DAY
(1993-2002)

experienced high fever and gastric distress during the trip, an illness which lasted about 36 hours and then passed quickly. The cost of the mission trip was provided by students' fees and the support of students' local churches; depending on the number of participants, expenses varied from $6000 to $10,000 per trip, including $3,000 to $5,000 in building materials. By 1995, the campus ministries were no longer working with Puentes de Christo, but with Ministerio de Fe (Faith Ministries) in McAllen, Texas and in the town of Miguel Aleman, across the border from Roma, TX. The work was done primarily in Miguel Aleman, where a strong relationship was developed with Pastor Hernandez, his wife Leticia and their children

The staff residents during 1994-1995 were Michael Hickerson, Rebecca Kerr, Eric D. Lopez, Ruben Mamani-Paco, Tripp Mullins, Betty Mutwiri, and Carmel Skeen.

Nine participants (Andy Oliver, Betty Mutwiri, Rebecca Kerr, Carmel Skeen, Kathryn Dowlen, Tripp Mullins, Gilbert Mamani-Paco, Eric Lopez, and Enoch Hendry) attended a National Ecumenical Christian Student Gathering in St. Louis during the Christmas-New Year's holiday, 1994-1995. They shared transportation with a group from the UTK Presbyterian Center. About the experience, Kathryn Dowlen wrote, in the March 1995 issue of *Wesley Wire*, "Before the conference I had no clue as to what to expect, but as I left St. Louis I was closer to understanding myself and my future in the celebration of Christian diversity across all barriers of distance, denomination, and culture. A wonderul way to start a new year." In the same issue, another student reported on the 1995 Spring Break mission trip as ".....eight days sleeping on floors, taking cold showers and eating simple meals...building affordable concrete block dwellings for the local population of Miguel Aleman, a border town south of McAllen, TX." Also in the March 1995 issue, Ross Owen, an

Ed.D. student, described the Graduate and Married Fellowship Supper held every other Tuesday evening

The annual Wesleyan Heritage trip was begun in spring 1995, during the Easter weekend break. A combination heritage tour and community building experience for students, the trips alternated between a drive through the Delaware Valley and a visit to Savannah, Georgia. In the Delaware Valley, stops included the first Methodist meeting house in the United States, as well as Francis Asbury's grave and sight-seeing in Baltimore, where the Wesley Foundation group shared an Easter Sunrise Service at Lovely Lane United Methodist Church, and enjoyed dinner at Obryki's Seafood House. They also toured the Babe Ruth Museum in the Inner Harbor. Twice, the Chorale sang at a Sunrise Service in the four years Baltimore was visited. In Savannah, they toured appropriate John Wesley sites relating to his time in the Anglican community in the 1730s. In the area, they stayed a large beach house at Tybee and attended the Sunrise Service on the Strand, and visited the United Methodist Church in Tybee where Enoch had been pastor earlier in his career. Favorite haunts were The Crab Shack and River Street in Savannah. One year, Christine (Chrissy) Machalik was baptized in the ocean at Tybee.

Beginning in winter 1995, Doris Teague of Newport, TN became the president of the Board of Directors, the first woman to serve in this position in the history of the Board. (Previously Doris had been instrumental in energizing her United Methodist Women's community to provide new draperies for the community room and other building improvements.) Elizabeth (Beth) Stivers, who had participated in two DISCIPLE groups during the 1980s, became secretary; Bruce Matthews was treasurer. Edward (Eddie) Dorn started work as seminary intern, program assistant and head resident in fall 1995, taking a year's leave from his studies at Duke Divinity School. The residential community was comprised of David Duvall, Beth Overbay, John Reviere, Sally Rowlett, and

A NEW DAY
(1993-2002)

Tim Smith. Other active leadership was provided by Ryan Kilpatrick, Carmel Skeen, Lisa Kay Phillips, Deanna Taylor, Michael Hickerson and Travis Hooper.

A new format for *Wesley Wire* began in fall 1995, and in its premiere issue repairs and renovations done to the Wesley Foundation building (provided by a 4-year grant from the Holston Conference Council on Ministries) were described – the waterproofing of the front and rear of the building below ground, repairing the water-damaged library, repairing and resurfacing the entire deck above the main building, repairing the wall and repainting the Community Room, the carpeting and repainting the Conference Room, and adding a handicapped access ramp and a new rail to the Chapel entrance. By fall 1995, the Wesley Foundation building had been in use for 28 years.

At a Board meeting on February 15, 1996, Enoch explained that of the $48,000 loan made for repairs, $10,000 had been repaid. It was announced that the Holston Conference treasurer was sending $7,000, to be applied both to the principal and interest, and would send equal payments for the principal's reduction over the next 12 months. Consequently, there was an urgent need for another special fund-raising effort to provide for continuing maintenance and repairs. Jeremy Morse agreed to chair a committee to organize the endeavor.

The Fall Retreat, October 13-15, 1995 was held at Sterchi Lodge, in conjunction with the College Class of Church Street United Methodist Church, at which time the guest speaker was Dr. Ron Hopson, an assistant professor of psychology at UTK.

The spring 1996 mission trip (March 15-23) again went to the border town of Miguel Aleman, providing labor to *Ministerio De Fe* (Faith Ministry), a church based ecumenical ministry operating in Mexico and McAllen, TX. *Wesley Wire* described the dimensions of the trip as "...an opportunity to learn and grow in faith, sharing an international and cross- cultural mission experience. Time for worship, conversation and reflection will be built into each evening's schedule. Students will be encouraged to share their experiences with friends and local faith communities upon our return." Each student participant paid $250 as a fee, and was encouraged to raise additional funds to make the trip possible. A financial appeal to alumni brought substantial gifts, including one from Dan B. Kelly, who was a UTK student from 1945-1949. Mr. Kelly contributed in memory of J. Irving McDonough, an example of the lasting influence of the Foundation on those whom it touched.

At work on the Mexican mission, 1996

The combined Wesley Foundation-Presbyterian participants in the spring 1996 mission trip were J.J. Rosenbaum, Susan Abernathy, Hajnalka Bardos, Grace Boyer, Bill Habicht, David

A NEW DAY
(1993-2002)

Duvall, Anne Peeples, Beth Overbay, Shelley Hall, Eddie Dorn, Ross Owen, Eddie Matos, Melynda Freeland, Daniel Boyd, Jason Shuppert, Mary Patterson, Camille Pedigo, Jason Rich, Laura Lee Rappe, Steve Musick and Enoch Hendry.

Mission work, Miguel Aleman, Mexico

The Spring production in 1996, the first in three years, was Archibald MacLeish's Pulitzer-Prize winning play, *J.B.*, which set the Book of Job in a modern context. Directed by Tim Smith, the play was described as examining the question of 'why bad things happen to good people' and 'how people deal with tragedies rather concentrating on the tragedies themselves.' Characterized as "a play in verse," the production was offered March 7-9 in the Robert Parrott Theatre. Included in the cast were Meredith Crosby, Eddie Dorn, David Farmer (J.B.), Anne Peeples, David Duvall, Tim Smith, Deanna Taylor, Jeanne Holder, Rebecca Phillips, Susan Hickerson, Travis Hooper, Eddie Matos, Sally Rowlett, Stacy Murray, and Enoch Hendry.

2

The Southeastern Jurisdictional Student Movement, growing after its re-birth, met in Knoxville on August 8-11, 1996. There was business conducted (elections, by-laws, future planning, etc.), but primarily students and campus ministers played, sang, studied and worshiped together. Speakers for the regional event included Don Shockley, from the United Methodist General Board of Campus Ministry and author of *Campus Ministry: The Church Beyond Itself,* and retired Bishop James Thomas.

Julius (J.B.) McCullough, a graduate student in biology, began a two-year tenure as head resident in fall 1996. The resident staff included Michelle Kent, Mary Patterson, Becky Phillips, and Tim Smith. Other students active in leadership roles were Terry Ryan, Becky Trammell, Julia Graves, David Farmer, Carmel Skeen, J.J. Rosenbaum, Camille Pedigo, John Riviere and Deanna Taylor. Thursday Luncheon was terminated, and a Wednesday Night Supper (prior to Vespers in the Chapel) was instituted. Other memorable events in the fall were a "Moon Over Melrose" Block Party, Wesleyan Heritage Classes ("Everything You Always Wanted To Know About The United Methodist Church But Didn't Know Whom To Ask"), a WHAM Halloween Party, an OXFAM fast – and football parking on home-game Saturdays.

B.J. McCullough and the WHAM kids, 1996

A NEW DAY
(1993-2002)

A Statement of Mission, which had been fashioned at the summer planning retreat, was adopted and circulated in fall 1996, declaring, "As a community of faith within the United Methodist Church, we of the Wesley Foundation....offer this statement of mission to clarify what we believe is God's purpose for us. The Wesley Foundation shall be not only a uniquely United Methodist Presence on the University of Tennessee, Knoxville campus, but also a dynamic Christian community of faith. This community shall worship God and serve others in the name of Jesus Christ. We will study the Bible and explore faith matters together in a spirit of love, joy, and fellowship, and challenge one another to strengthen our faith. This community will strive to celebrate its diversity and integrity through reconciliation, trust and unconditional love. All this we will do in order to create a harmonious environment in which to share our walk of faith."

On December 8, 1996, at Sunday Morning Worship, the Wesley Foundation Chorale presented a Christmas Cantata, "a Service of Advent and Coming," with liturgists Michelle Kent, David Duvall, David Farmer and Allison Bassett. The accompanist was Ruth Lovell. Enoch's homily was entitled "Settling Accounts."

In conjunction with other UTK campus ministries, the Wesley Foundation participated in a CROP WALK in April 1997, a 10 kilometer (6.2 mile) walk through the campus to raise funds for the hunger arm of Church World Service and as an act of solidarity. Since more than half the world's population have only their feet as transportation, campus walkers echoed the words of the CROP WALK motto, "We walk because they walk." A total of $350.00 was raised, allocated both to Church World Service and to the Knoxville Love Kitchen.

Worries about finances and funding concerned the Board of Directors increasingly in 1996-1997. It was reported that funding

THE SHINING OF LIGHT: A HISTORY OF THE WESLEY FOUNDATION
AT THE UNIVERSITY OF TENNESSEE, 1922-2007

'CROP WALK,' 1997

from the Holston Annual Conference for its several Wesley Foundations was likely to continue to decrease, and supporting Districts had reached their maximum in support. It seemed probable that some Conference Wesley Foundations would shift to a half-time basis, and one might be closed. These concerns highlighted the urgency for the UTK Wesley Foundation to find new and different ways of developing financial support, but perennial difficulties shadowed finding the right means to achieve the goal. At least since 1943, when the first Center was purchased, adequate funding had been a struggle; now, the issue was reaching survival proportions.

Tim Smith directed the spring production of 1997, *Arsenic and Old Lace,* a classic Broadway play by Joseph Kesselring. The cast was comprised of Allison Bassett, Jack Blair, Mason Brown,

A NEW DAY
(1993-2002)

Dan Cragan, Matthew Dobson, Jeanne Holder, Dan Kelley, Michelle Kent, Michelle Morse, Camille Pedigo, Becky Phillips, Sally Rowlett, Tim Smith, Deanna Taylor and Enoch Hendry.

Arsenic and Old Lace, **1997**

A festive week-end was organized in fall 1997 to celebrate the 30th anniversary of the opening of the Wesley Foundation building. On Saturday, September 27, a cook-out and informal reception drew alumni, parents, students and friends, and there was a celebratory Sunday Morning Worship on September 28 in the Theatre. A luncheon followed in the Community Room. Honored guests included the second full-time campus minister Glen Otis (Curly) Martin, who had led the Foundation from 1951-1960, and his wife Margaret (Marge), from Lexington Park, Maryland. Also present were Bob Parrott and his wife Donna. Telephone and mail greetings were received from alumni who had been involved in the Foundation's ministry in years past, including Jack Looney of Crossville, TN who had served as the Council president for the

THE SHINING OF LIGHT: A HISTORY OF THE WESLEY FOUNDATION
AT THE UNIVERSITY OF TENNESSEE, 1922-2007

academic year 1958-1959. At the Sunday Morning Worship 30th anniversary celebration, Becky Trammell was the accompanist, and David Duvall was liturgist. The hymn "Morning Has Broken" was accompanied by Paul Wright, Sheryl Lawrence Howard, and Dan Cragan. The Chorale's anthem was "Come Thou Fount of Every Blessing," directed by John Reviere. As an offertory, the original music was "Untitled" by Dan Cragan, with Dan on synthesizer, Sheryl L. Howard, oboe, and Michelle Kent, flute. Bob Parrott's sermon entitled "More Than Bricks and Mortar" sought to celebrate the light which had shown from the Wesley Foundation not only during the 30 years of the present building's existence, but throughout its entire 75 years of history.

Julius McCullough continued his work as head resident in 1997-1998. The resident staff included Jack Blair, Matt Dobson, Michelle Kent, Stacey Murray, Tim Smith, Deanna Taylor, and Tiffany Thomas. Among the group actively participating in core leadership were Austin Adkinson, David Duvall, Meredith Crosby, David Farmer, Ryan Kilpatrick, Andy Kneeland, Jeremy Shuppert, Amy Shuppert, Sally Rowlett, Camille Pedigo, Jeanne Holder, Allison Bassett, Jennifer Cloar, Jaimie McMahon, Teresa Bridges, and Jason Shuppert. Opportunities for worship and study were highlighted by Sunday Morning Worship, Wednesday Vespers, DISCIPLE Bible study, Galileo (the Bennett Horton Discussion Group), and the Wesleyan Heritage Study. Continuing service projects (among others) were WHAM, the Tim Kerin Canned Food Drive, work with Habitat for Humanity, and a Hunger Awareness Week.

The service of candle lighting, long a Wesley Foundation tradition, continued to be one of the most significant events of the ministry's development. On December 3, 1997, in the Chapel, Meredith Crosby read Scripture (Luke 2:1-21), Jeremy Shuppert offered special music, John Reviere led the Chorale in "Come Thou Long Expected Jesus," and David Farmer concluded with the

A NEW DAY
(1993-2002)

Canticle of Light and Darkness. The warmth of transcendence --as candles in the recessed niches of the apse and lighted candles held by congregants slowly dispelled the darkness and then illuminated the entire Chapel -- was a unique December time. *Grace* became not a pious word or a doctrine or an item of belief, but an experience of God's presence.

Financial concerns continued to be critical in the fall of 1997. A letter to potential contributors specified that the Holston Conference's support (although cut from previous levels) provided the yearly "fair share" amount of almost $100,000 to the UTK Wesley Foundation budget, and that the combined Knoxville, Maryville and Morristown Districts provided more than $30,000 yearly. In addition, the active students (through car parking, worship offering and program fees) contributed another $25,000 yearly. These combined funds still did not provide the level of support needed to maintain the strength of the program, and parents, alumni and friends were asked to contribute an additional $20,000.

Sunday Morning Worship, in the Chapel, continued to be a lynchpin of the Foundation's ministry. Some of Enoch Hendry's sermon titles, during 1997-1998, were "Lessons From a Sidewalk Crack," "Human Shortcomings," "Living Like the Widow – And Other Foolish Notions," "The Far Side of Complexity," "Slapping God's Wrist," "Down the Mountain and Back to Town," "Random Kindnesses and Senseless Acts of Beauty," "Word Keepers," and "Counting the Cost of Our Impatience." The interactive nature of the worship continued: the gospel lesson was read aloud by members of the congregation, the peace was shared, and the benediction – with the *a capella* chorus – sent the congregation forth.

The spring production for 1998 was *The Importance of Being Earnest,* by Oscar Wilde. A British comedy of manners, it was presented in the Theatre on March 6-8 and March 13-15.

The Importance of Being Earnest, **1998**

The annual Spring Break mission trip to Northern Mexico was held on March 21-28, 1998. Once again, the group provided labor in the town of Miguel Aleman for Ministerio De Fe, an ecumenical ministry operating in Mexico from a base in McAllen, TX. They constructed concrete block dwellings for local residents. The project was "ecumenical in design, cross-cultural in scope, and labor-intensive." A combined work force of 40 John XIII, Presbyterian and Wesley Foundation participants were housed in a church building, sleeping on concrete floors, taking cold showers and eating simple meals.

A NEW DAY
(1993-2002)

3

Beginning in fall 1998, the musical dimension of both Sunday Morning Worship and Vespers was enriched when two fine musicians, David Peeples (a music major and accomplished bassist) and Jeremy Shuppert (a fine guitarist and song-writer) collaborated as accompanists and performers. David Duvall, Tim Smith and John Reviere had already begun as The Trio, performing *a capella* vocal harmony pieces in both services, as well as performing in area congregations. The Trio produced a CD of the music they performed at the Wesley Foundation, entitled *Big Iron Cross*, named to interpret the wrought-iron cross hanging *in medias res* over the altar in the Chapel. The CD cover featured a photograph of the chapel with the cross as its central focus, enriched by Hugh C. Tyler's original hand-painted Flemish ceiling and cross beams.

The Board of Directors worked diligently on the need for additional fund raising. A phone-a-thon and other methods were explored, including a video to be used for money raising efforts. The ominous possibility loomed that the entire heating- air conditioning system needed repair, expected to cost $75,000. Maintaining the 30-year-old building became increasingly a major issue at Board meetings.

Three students, Tim Smith, Matt Dobson and John Reviere, who were planning to graduate from the University in 1999, originated the idea of a "Senior Gift," their project the landscaping the front lawn near the parking lot. The Chorale, under John Reviere's leadership, increased in size, and continued to visit churches and charges to sing and share the ministry of the Wesley Foundation. Timothy L. Bagwell was the head resident in 1998-1999; members of the resident staff were Raquel Bagwell, Austin Adkinson, Jeff Baker, Jack Blair, Dagan Coppock, Jennifer Herrig, David Peeples, and Christina Shaver. Other active students

THE SHINING OF LIGHT: A HISTORY OF THE WESLEY FOUNDATION
AT THE UNIVERSITY OF TENNESSEE, 1922-2007

included Tim Smith, Tiffany Thomas, Meredith Crosby, John Reviere, Matt Dobson, Eric Crowe, Jeff Baker, Larson Cook, Stacey Murray, Michelle Kent, Jaimie McMahon, Allen Cain, and Sjon-Paul Conyer.

In 1999, another Spring Break mission trip was made on behalf of the residents of Mission Miguel Aleman in northern Mexico, again working with Ministerio de Fe, defined as "a ministry of compassion, based on the Love of our Lord Jesus Christ, in responding to the spiritual, physical, housing and other needs of the people that live in the Texas/Mexico Border area." An ecumenical work force of 31 people participated.

For the campus, the value of the mission trip was recognized by the University as a "recommended" alternative Spring Break Opportunity.

A resounding success was *The Cotton Patch Gospel,* the spring production presented March 4-7, 1999. Written by Tom Key

The cast of *The Cotton Patch Gospel*, 1999

A NEW DAY
(1993-2002)

and Russell Treyz, accompanied by music by Harry Chapin, the musical was a Southern vernacular re-telling of the Matthew gospel story. A cast of 30 acted, sang and danced to a 5-piece Bluegrass band featuring Jeremy Shuppert and David Peeples. Enoch Hendry pronounced it one of the highlights of his tenure as campus minister. The weekend of the spring production became Parents' Day, which included a reception, an invitation to the play, and a pancake breakfast prior to Sunday Morning Worship.

Finances – and even institutional survival -- continued to be a rising concern. For the first time in six years, the Holston Conference awarded the UTK Wesley Foundation a yearly increase in Fair Share giving in the amount of $111,000.

The residential community in 1999-2000 included Jack Blair, head resident; Jose Alfaro, Austin Adkinson, Matt Dobson, Jennifer Herrig, David Peeples, Allison Pearce, and Jeremy Shuppert.

4

A recognition of the highest order was awarded to Enoch Hendry in 1999 when he was named "Campus Minister of The Year" by the United Methodist Foundation for Christian Higher Education. The award was officially announced at a special event of celebration at the Wesley Foundation. The nomination for the award was made by Carol Wilson, a member of the Wesley Foundation Board, through the Holston Conference Board of Higher Education. The affirmation of Enoch's style of ministry and his accomplishments was an event of great significance not only for himself but for the UTK Wesley Foundation. The award provided $5000 for new program initiatives at the Wesley Foundation. That January (1999) Enoch traveled with a Witness for Peace delegation (including five Wesley Foundation students) to Managua, Nicaragua, where they spent nine days "learning -- and digging latrines."

5

By spring 1999, four scholarships had long been established through the Wesley Foundation, or by recommendation of the UTK campus minister. The Bob and Donna Parrott Scholarship, given by Bryan, Beth and Andrea Jackson, had been established in 1980 ".....to recognize contributions by students to the ongoing ministry of the Wesley Foundation...and in appreciation for and in recognition of all that Bob and Donna have meant to those of us who love them." Beginning in the academic year 1980-1981, those receiving this scholarship by 1999-2000 had been Danna Carter, Edward W. Tucker, Michael Bender, Lorri Crump, Deane Young, Sheryl Lawrence, William A. Hunt, Lynne M. Dunn, Kwame Agyenim-Boateng, Marty Seals, Julia Morse, Dana Truitt, Anna Brown, Joe Pyle, J. Robert McLeary, Cheryl Mobley, Travis Hooper, Beth Overbay, John Reviere, Tim Smith, David Farmer, Larson Cook and Stacey Murray.

The Marian W. Eastridge Memorial Scholarship, funded from 1983-1993 by alumni Charles and Kay Arrants Short of Ithaca, NY, was given in memory of alumna Marian Wilson Eastridge. Recipients included Mel Stripling, Jay Kaiser, Sheung Shih Chia, Lynne M. Dunn, Dawn Traynor, Valerie Ireson, Richard Irwin, Wes Fanning, and – in 1992-1993 -- Ruben Mamani-Paco of Bolivia, son of Bishop Zacharias Mamani, the United Methodist bishop of Bolivia.

The Irvin J. McDonough Memorial Scholarship, which was technically a UTK special scholarship, was funded by Mrs. Evelyn McDonough and her son J. Duggins McDonough, widow and son of "Mr. Mack," the first full-time campus minister. The recipient is

A NEW DAY
(1993-2002)

named by recommendation each spring by the UTK campus minister.

The Robert E. Parrott Theology Award, begun in spring 1992, was initiated as a means of encouragement and support for active Wesley Foundation students to pursue theological study at a United Methodist seminary. Recipients have been John D. Wadhams, Theta Wagner-Miller, Alan J. Cloar, Joe Pyle, Jack Blair and Mel Stripling.

6

The Wesleyan Heritage Trip to the Georgia Sea Islands (Savannah, Savannah Beach and St. Simons Island) during the 1999 Easter weekend gave students an opportunity to see John Wesley's first (and only) American parish, the United Methodist Museum at Epworth by the Sea, and Fort Frederica where Charles Wesley lived and worked. Among those students included in the trip were David Duvall, David Farmer, Lawson Cook, Allen Cain, Will Pedigo, Matt Dobson, Jack Blair, Tim Bagwell, Christine Michalik, Jan Conley, Jaimie McMahon, Jeff Baker, Jennifer Herrig, Jennifer Cloar, Alisha Luna, Jason Sanks, Adam Fiscar, J.J. Rosenbaum, and Marty Woodlee.

Meredith Leigh Crosby was the head resident during the academic year 2000-2001; the resident staff was comprised of Jose Alfaro, Kristen Burkhart, Jennifer Herrig, Kevin McCasland, Stephanie Messer, Christine Michalik, and David Peeples. Terri McBee and Sam Mason continued to serve as vital members of the Foundation's staff. Continuing program events for the year were highlighted – DISCIPLE Bible Study, Galileo, Brown Bag Bible Browser, and the Married and Graduate Student Fellowship. Fall events featured a Cades Cove Hike, a Labor Day Picnic and an October Hay Ride. Enoch Hendry described the year's program as focused on worship. "We worship twice as week, averaging almost

THE SHINING OF LIGHT: A HISTORY OF THE WESLEY FOUNDATION
AT THE UNIVERSITY OF TENNESSEE, 1922-2007

90 on Sunday mornings and near 50 on Wednesday Evenings. Our 22 voice Chorale provides special music for our community. We have four ongoing study groups including our eleventh annual class of DISCIPLE Bible study. Our extraordinary drama group, the Wesley Players, offers two presentations annually, a simple Christmas theme performance in the late fall and a full-blown fully-staged play in the winter....Our building houses eight students who are the core of our leadership team. These folk, organized as a Covenant Discipleship Team, are critical to our commitment to train leaders for this generation of United Methodists."

The spring production of 2000 was *The Foreigner,* a play by Larry Shue, directed by Tim Smith. Travis Beacham was assistant director, and Julia Carter was the stage manager. At the time of the production, the air conditioning system and other mechanical systems in the building were functioning only on a minimal level, but the ministry flourished. Students participated in a tutoring mission on Monday evenings at Virginia Avenue United Methodist Church. WHAM at Wesley House continued three days a week with a tutoring program.

On February 21, 2001, Tim Kobler, chairperson of the Board of Directors, and Lynn Hutton, treasurer, reported the continual struggle with the budget in the face of heating and air conditioning system needs, as well as the heavy insurance loads carried. When the Board met on April 19, 2001, the Building and Grounds report sounded an ominous note: ".....The boiler is dead. Patching it could cost up to $20,000 per year. The total cost of the recommendations from Perfection Services of Knoxville.....is $75,000." After much discussion, the proposal of the firm Perfection Services Company was accepted. The installation of the new system initiated further discussion concerning the securing of financing.

A NEW DAY
(1993-2002)

The 2001 Mexico Mission Trip at Spring Break concentrated on the construction of homes and a clinic, with a party for the children of the community of Miguel Aleman. Another Heritage Trip to Georgia celebrated the heritage of Methodists in the New World of the eighteenth century.

The spring production for 2001 was Tom Stoppard's *Rosencrantz & Guildenstern Are Dead,* starring Jan Conley as Rosencrantz and Colin Fisher as Guildenstern. John Sides played the role of Hamlet, and Mike Adams was Polonius. Jaimie McMahon played Gertrude. Travis Beacham was the director, and Julia Carter the stage manager. Kristi Maxwell, a staff writer for the *Daily Beacon,* reported Travis Beacham's comments on the play, "It is a fantastic play on its own account, but it is also a source of material for many literature classes...The characters Rosencrantz and Guildenstern have an interesting stance because they do not leave the stage over the course of the play. They are blessed or cursed with a fantastic majority of the stage time, and they have been more an up to the challenge."

7

Fall 2001 was overshadowed by the terrorist attack on the World Trade Center in New York, and – like the entire UTK campus -- the Wesley Foundation was directly changed. The worlds of previous campus generations, from the early 1920s to the late 1990s, were overshadowed. A new age suddenly began. On Tuesday, September 11, 2001 Enoch Hendry met with Vice President for Student Affairs Tim Rogers and others to plan a memorial service at Thompson Boling Arena for Thursday evening. As a voice among student and faculty voices that night, Enoch was invited to give the central address at the event, an experience which he long remembered as a unique opportunity.

Meredith Crosby continued as head resident during 2001-2002. The resident staff members were Jason Sanks, Julia Wall, Don Petty, Kirk Lowe, Jose Alfaro, Sara Higgins, and Stephanie Messer. Active in the work of the Coordinating Cabinet were Yvonne Jones, John Sides, Jason Sanks, Don Petty, Jaimie McMahon, Stephanie Messer, Alan Cain, Candace Kear, Allie Baxter, Sara Higgins, and Julia Wall. Highlights of the years were a Halloween Dance, participation in Habitat for Humanity, Scarf Day (in which women wear scarves – or men wear arm bands -- to show support for Muslims on campus), the Tim Kerin Canned Food Drive, a joint retreat with the Lutheran Campus ministries, and the December candle lighting service. After flagrant disregard of the Wesley Foundation's "No Alcohol" policy during football game parking in the parking lot, a new emphasis on appropriate behavior on Foundation property was declared, with an announcement that continued failure to abide by the policy would result in the immediate revocation of parking privileges and the forfeiture of all future opportunities to use the grounds during UTK football games.

In early 2002, Enoch Hendry announced his decision to accept the pastorate of historic Trinity United Methodist Church in Savannah in the South Georgia Conference, which had remained his home Annual Conference. He expressed to the Board his personal difficulty in leaving and his appreciation for the support he had received. The beginning date of his new position in Savannah was July 1, 2002. The timing of the decision and the announcement offered only a short period of time in which a search for a new Wesley Foundation campus minister could be developed. There was resounding gratitude – from Board members and students and others -- for Enoch's gifts and dedication.

The 2002 spring production was *Honk! A Musical Tale of 'The Ugly Duckling',* the book and lyrics by Anthony Drewe and music by George Stiles, presented April 5,6,12,13,and 14. Also in

A NEW DAY
(1993-2002)

2002, *Superstars: A Presentation of Talent by the Wesley Foundation Community* was offered. Participating in the production were David Peeples, John Sides, Dustin Garvey, Jan Conley, Jaimie McMahon, Jason Sanks, Jan Conley, Don Petty, Michael Adams, Allison Baxter, Derrick Bellamy, Yvonne Jones, and the Wesley Foundation Chorale.

In his last written report to the Board of Directors on April 18, 2002, Enoch highlighted the 2001-2002 year emphasizing the work of the Coordinating Cabinet, Sunday Morning Worship, the Wednesday fellowship meal, Bible Study (including a new group entitled General B.S. [General Bible Study], the Wesleyan Heritage trip, and service projects. "Due to a variety of reasons, what would have been our Ninth Annual Mission Trip to Miguel Aleman in Mexico was canceled. While this was quite personally disappointing, the plans to bring our host family to Knoxville this weekend will provide our community the closure we had anticipated to this long standing mission initiative." He commented on the burden of paying the loan for the HVAC (Heating, Ventilation, Air Conditioning) system. "...We have been very close and careful regarding expenditure of funds each month. It is increasingly critical that we look at alternative fund raising practices. As new changes are to be worked in our Annual Conference relationship a proactive posture toward securing needed funds (especially for building maintenance) is important. Let's work hard to make sure that Holston knows what is needed and what should be done. This building is an extraordinary asset to our program and to the Conference. All of us need to do our part to ensure its survival." He concluded with special accolades for custodian Sam Mason and for administrative assistant Terri McBee.

Enoch Hendry's tenure of nine years as the UTK Wesley Foundation's campus minister was an era of accomplishment and enthusiasm. In the words of Harvey C. Brown, the original hero of the early Knoxville student community, Enoch had indeed left "deep tracks" in its life and history.

Wesleyan Heritage Trip, Savannah, GA, 1997

Chapter XI

IN A NEW WORLD
(2002-2007)

1

By the earliest years of the 21st century, the new UTK world -- having been shifting firmly into place since the late 1970s -- represented a remarkable change from the campus of the 1920s when the nucleus Wesley Foundation began, an age which still bore some of the marks of the late 19th century. The new world was also vastly different from the 1930s-style campus of 1942, when the first full-time Wesley Foundation ministry started, or from the turbulence of the 1960s. The transformed era had now become a new universe of scientific technologies, computerized information systems, automation, televised lectures, a widening curriculum, a growing internationalism, a greatly expanded geographical area of campus buildings and parking garages, multiple legions of student and faculty automobiles, the daily search for parking spaces, and the availability of a Starbucks café within the Undergraduate Library. There were radical shifts in student and faculty lifestyles. Internet installations in residence hall rooms had become standard housing equipment. There were ubiquitous signs of change in student gear -- cell-phones and laptops and blackberries and ipods and backpacks. T-shirts and walking shorts and flip-flops had become the new warm weather dress code. Classes and parties were now attended by those who had grown up in the wake of the sexual revolution, in a world of HIV and AIDS consciousness. While the campus was still relatively conservative in many ways, it was now populated by those who held increasingly diverging views of education, leisure, work, sex, money, commitments, patriotism, spirituality, the Church, the world and truth.

THE SHINING OF LIGHT: A HISTORY OF THE WESLEY FOUNDATION
AT THE UNIVERSITY OF TENNESSEE, 1922-2007

In this swiftly changing environment, Lauri Jo Cranford – the first woman campus minister in the history of the UTK Wesley Foundation -- was appointed to the position, beginning July 1, 2002. A graduate of Candler School of Theology, she had previously served as Associate Pastor of First United Methodist Church in Oak Ridge, TN.

Michael (Mike) Adams became head resident in fall 2002, followed (in 2003) by Jose Alfaro. Rowland Buck became the chairman of the Board of Directors; Lynn Hutton continued as treasurer. At one of the first Board meetings of the new era of 2002, building needs were discussed – heating problems in the residents' area, roofing problems which needed attention, the issue of necessary handicap access (with estimates ranging from $5,000 to $10,000), and the urgent need for repair of the Chapel window. The problem of Conference and District and alumni fund raising continued to be of urgent concern. There were plans underway to "restart" Bible study and to plan for another Mexico mission trip during Spring Break 2003. In addition to Michael Adams, students present for the September 5, 2002 meeting of the Board were Jose Alfaro, Allison Baxter, Stephanie Messer and John Sides.

Lauri Jo Cranford

At another Board meeting, on November 14, 2002, there was consideration of a new packet of Wesley Foundation By-Laws which were amended and accepted. There was discussion about the responsibilities of the new Holston Conference Personnel Resources Team, and about a provision in the By-Laws indicating that elected Board members with two unexcused absences from regularly scheduled meetings were subject to being removed from the roster of active members. There was a redefinition of the responsibilities of the Board and of the campus minister. Four-year panels of elected Board members were established, including clergy and lay representatives of the three supporting Districts and the Holston Conference, UTK faculty and staff, alumni/ae of the Wesley Foundation ministry, and "at least two or three students currently involved in the campus ministry." Program issues noted at the meeting were the renaming of the Galileo discussion group because of its change of mission to an arts endeavor, and the planning of Advent-Christmas activities -- and that the goal of 30 participants in the Spring Break mission trip to Mexico had been set. It was reported that a new building maintenance contract had been entered into with Perfection Heating and Cooling Company of Knoxville and that fire code concerns had been identified.

Other activities in fall 2002 included N.A.G. (Nameless Arts Group), a Cades Cove Hayride (organized by Derrick Bellamy), men's and women's groups, Wesley House Outreach (work in the Mechanicsville area defined as an "after school tutoring program for elementary-aged kids"), and the Chorale. Sunday Morning Worship in the Chapel continued. Accompanists for the services included Becky Goemaat and John Sides. Among the liturgists presiding were Jaimie McMahon, Allison Baxter, Jason Sanks, Michael Adams, Jan Conley, and Russ Dunlap. Activities noted in the Sunday worship bulletins included work with the congregation of Virginia Avenue United Methodist Church, Wednesday night suppers and Vespers, and Friday Night Stuff. In January 2003, students participated in Divine Rhythm, a Holston Conference event in Gatlinburg, featuring "a well-known speaker, music, worship and "time together."

A production of Terrence McNally's *Corpus Christi* at the All Campus Theatre, the UTK student-run theatre company, on February 1, 2, 4-8, 2003 caused only a small stir on the campus. The play, a gay-themed retelling of the story of Christ, had received death threats in Los Angeles and London, but – as expressed by play critic Doug Mason for *The Knoxville News-Sentinel* -- it received an "immaculate reception" in Knoxville. The play was discussed in depth by the Campus Ministers' Council, and at least one member of the Council found the play "offensive." Lauri Jo Cranford reported that she planned to read the play before seeing it, and to see the play with a group of students. She said, "It has a powerful message. It's beautifully written. There are certain scenes that are painful...(but) they add a power to the original Christ story......People can't seem to get past the 'Jesus could not have been gay' issue. They can't get past that enough to hear what the play is really saying."

Because of funding problems, the Spring Break mission trip to Miguel Aleman in Mexico did not materialize. Instead, in March 2003, the Wesley Foundation community worked in an Appalachian Service Project in Southwest Virginia. Participants included Stephanie Messer, Michael Adams, Kirk Lowe, James Hughes, Russell Dunlap, Jose Alfaro, Neal Charlton, Lindsey Lands, David Herzog, Leslie Hamilton and Lauri Jo Cranford.

A Day-Long Peace Vigil was held at the Wesley Foundation on April 2, 2003 in order "to mourn the loss of human life, to pray for peace and compassion, and to support our troops overseas." Flyers distributed on campus announced that the Foundation Chapel would be open from 9 a.m. until midnight, with special services at noon and 7:30 p.m.

The Foundation's 2003 Spring production was *The Laramie Project,* a dramatic work by Moises Kaufman and the Tectonic Theater Project, presented on April 4, 5, 6, 10, 11 and 13. An ambitious and creative production, it was directed by John Sides. There were roundtable discussions following every production except on April 10. The cast featured Mike Adams, Jan Conley, Leigh Hruby, Deanna McGovern, Grant Rhodes, Jay Schaad, Kip Williams and Tracy Windeknecht. In a letter to area youth group leaders, Lauri Jo Cranford wrote: ".....This play focuses on a community's reaction to the beating and death of

IN A NEW WORLD
(2002-2007)

Matthew Shepherd, a student in Laramie, Wyoming, a young gay man…..The purpose of the play is not to make Matthew Shepherd a hero or to convince anyone that homosexuality is acceptable or not acceptable. Rather, this play focuses on how hate crimes can and do affect us all." In an interview for an article in *The Daily Beacon,* she commented to the campus, "In a time when we are often told that teenagers and young adults don't care about the world around them, or are only concerned with themselves, I hope you can experience something different. This play has been and continues to be an act of love, passion and compassion for those students involved…We as Christians are to spread the news of hope, a hope that is found in Christ's love for us and presence with us in times of trials…As a Christian community, part of our responsibility and calling is to build one another up and to love another."

Sunday Morning Worship continued in the Chapel during the academic year 2002-2003. The liturgy included the Lighting of the Altar Candles, a Call to Worship, an Opening Prayer, Hymns, the Witness to the Spirit, the Peace, an Affirmation of Faith, the Scripture Lesson, the Meditation (offered by Lauri Jo Cranford and others), and the traditional Choral Benediction.

2

Life in a Wesley Foundation is never exempt from tensions and internal strife, the manifestation of which represents a challenge to those trying to build a community of faith. The fair, open exchange of ideas and beliefs, even in an environment of academic freedom, is not easy to achieve. At times there are sharply conflicting perspectives. Such tensions had been present in the UTK campus ministry since its beginning, including disagreements between Board members, between Board members and the campus minister, between the campus minister and students and between groups of students. As in the experience of

THE SHINING OF LIGHT: A HISTORY OF THE WESLEY FOUNDATION
AT THE UNIVERSITY OF TENNESSEE, 1922-2007

any group of gathered Christians, patience and tolerance and courage on all sides are needed if resolutions are to be found.

In 2002-2003, such tensions included problems which had arisen among staff members. A personality conflict developed between Lauri Jo Cranford and Terri McBee, the administrative assistant. Terri was dismissed abruptly from her position by the Board's Executive Committee on April 16, 2003. Since Terri had been an admired presence and staff member for 16 years, the dismissal caused a severe crisis for a group of students within the Wesley Foundation community as well as among alumni who had worked with Terri.

Although there was a strong affirmation of Lauri Jo's style of leadership from some students, tensions with other students grew, particularly within the Coordinating Cabinet and the residential staff. Major differences in program emphasis and points of view were manifested, differences which finally became counterproductive. A casualty of the situation was a marked diminution of the on-going ministry. Kirk Lowe, who had been slated to become the head resident for 2003-2004, chose not to accept the position, and the formation of a student staff community (for 2003-2004) loomed as a significant problem. The Board made a decision to close the residential program for the coming year, and to use the time to make needed repairs and renovations to the ground floor quarters, and to reassess the status of the student staff.

Sidney (Sid) Collins, the chair of the Board of Directors following Rowland Buck's resignation in April 2003, presided over a meeting of the Board (on December 11, 2003) to discuss the issue of the staff residents' role in the Wesley Foundation ministry. Under consideration were the questions of student leadership and the strategic value and costs of a residential presence in the building. It was agreed that, when the resident staff program resumed, the responsibilities of the head resident and the

IN A NEW WORLD
(2002-2007)

community of residents needed further clarification, and that an appraisal should be made of the role of student leadership. In the background of the crisis was the long evolution of students' involvement in Wesley Foundation decision-making concerning program, beginning at least with the early 1950s and in the campus tumult of the 1960s. Student representatives at this crucial discussion included Russell Dunlap, Jaimie McMahon, and Betzy Elifrits.

In 2003-2004, the Wesley Foundation experienced a significant juncture. Issues were faced. The community moved forward in the new, changing world.

The Wesley Foundation Chapel

THE SHINING OF LIGHT: A HISTORY OF THE WESLEY FOUNDATION
AT THE UNIVERSITY OF TENNESSEE, 1922-2007

3

At the June 2004 session of the Holston Annual Conference in Lake Junaluska, NC, Lauri Jo Cranford was appointed as Associate Pastor of the Munsey Memorial United Methodist Church in Johnson City. David R. Jackson, who had earned a Master of Business Administration degree from the University of Tennessee in 1993 and a Master of Divinity degree from Candler School of Theology (Emory University) in 2000, became the campus minister at the Wesley Foundation, beginning work on July 1, 2004. Previously, he had served Holston Conference churches at Philadelphia, St. Paul's East (Knoxville), and as the Associate Pastor at Wesley Memorial United Methodist Church in Johnson City. In the 82 years of the Foundation's life, he was the seventh full-time campus minister.

David Jackson

At a meeting of the Board of Directors on August 2, 2004, David Jackson introduced himself and his views of ministry by explicating the "Four Fs – Folks, Facility, Finances and Faithfulness." These motifs became his interpretive signature. It was agreed that Mark Clifton, skilled in both traditional and contemporary music, was to be hired as worship leader. Eva Cowell as administrative assistant and Sam Mason as custodian continued their service to the Wesley Foundation. Betzy Elifrits was confirmed as secretary of the Board. Concerns about finishing

IN A NEW WORLD
(2002-2007)

much-needed phase two of the HVAC system were discussed, the cost announced as approximately $25,000. Repairs on the building's slate roof also claimed priority, for which a new "Raise the Roof" capital campaign was planned. As a major program concern, attendance at Sunday Morning Worship had decreased sharply during 2003-2004, and it was announced that beginning in fall 2004, Sunday worship would be re-scheduled on Sunday evenings, preceded by a Sunday supper.

The academic year 2004-2005 was a year of redirection in the new world. Among active students were Jon Rowland, Will Pearson, Rachel Carvell, Lindsey Lands, Blake Renfro, Jay Smith, Russ Dunlap, Will Penner, and Jessica Torrance. The schedule of fall activities highlighted a Halloween Party for the Wesley House Community Center, active Friday Night Stuff, work with the Hunger Committee and Extra Help programs, and a political debate and movie night. The Wesley Foundation choir was re-activated, with help from Board member and alumna Sheryl L. Howard. Faith-based activities, such as Bible study, were slower to re-activate. The newly organized residential community had begun to work efficiently. After a period of adjustment, the new time for Sunday worship was well received, rearranged with supper (provided by area United Methodist Women's groups) and small groups following. David Jackson and seven students were part of a Church Street United Methodist work crew which traveled to Mexico during Spring Break 2005.

Active student leadership for the next year, 2005-2006, included Sunny Larkin (director of the Chorale), Eric Reagan (pianist), Blake Renfro, Trevor Renfro, Jon Rowland, Russ Dunlap, L.A. McCrae, Betzy Elifrits, Eric Doolittle and Jessica Torrance. Brandon Wright became the Student Intern, assisting the campus minister with coordination and communication of activities. Mel Stripling was elected to be chair of the Board of Directors, the second Wesley Foundation alumnus to occupy the position; Stacey Murray became vice-chair. In August 2006, Anne-Marie Tugwell was named treasurer. The resignation of Sam Mason, custodian extraordinaire, was received by the Board with many expressions of appreciation for his fifteen years of efficient and devoted work. Jon Rowland was hired as the temporary custodian for summer 2006.

A full program of student activities continued in 2005-2006, with Sunday night worship and supper, Wednesday night dinner and discussion, Friday Night Stuff, Bible Study and small group meetings. A mission trip to the Mississippi Gulf Coast (to the Biloxi-D'Iberville area) offered students an opportunity to participate in post-Katrina re-building. Among other highlights was Divine Rhythm in January, an alumni weekend in April, and Parents' Weekend.

In fall 2006, Heather Godsey, an ordained Disciples of Christ clergywoman who had previous campus ministry experience at Case-Western University in Cleveland, OH, joined the staff of the Wesley Foundation on a part-time basis, with special responsibility for a women's Bible study group, assistance with the music ministry, and the task of building relationships with students. When Eva Cowell, administrative assistant, accepted a teaching position at UTK, her office duties were consequently shared by Heather and David. A colorful ministry brochure for 2006-2007 announced the several areas of activity – mission trips, local mission opportunities, Bible study and small group discussion, a traditional Sunday Worship on Sundays at 6:45 p.m. followed by an evening meal (provided by area United Methodist Women), the United Methodist Heritage Trip, Friday Night Stuff, and other "entertainment-distractions." A highlight of the 2006-2007 academic year was an Iron Chef competition in April, and another Spring Break mission trip to Biloxi and to D'Iberville, MS.

IN A NEW WORLD
(2002-2007)

Because of age and recurring water damage, the Wesley Foundation's library – which had needed thoroughgoing repair for years – underwent a major gutting and renovation, including the resealing of the front interior wall and the installation of a new wood floor and the purchase of new library furniture. Students provided much of the skilled work on the project. Maintained on an inside wall was the plaster frieze *Cantoria,* which had originally been set into the living room fireplace arrangement of the McDowell house in 1906. The renovation, at a cost of approximately $20,000, returned the library to the full, inviting usefulness it had not experienced since the late 1960s, shortly after the building was opened.

At an Alumni Weekend in April 2007, Enoch Hendry preached at a special Sunday Morning Worship in the Chapel. Bob Parrott spoke at the dinner on the previous night, emphasizing the Wesley Foundation's evolving ministry on the UTK campus. During the week-end, Ann Curry, a skilled needlewoman, presented to the Wesley Foundation one of the most remarkable gifts it had ever received -- new, hand-sewn chancel kneeling cushions for the Chapel, which repeated the shields, symbols, stars and border designs originally painted by Hugh C. Tyler on the Chapel ceiling and beams in 1957.

4

On June 12, 2007, during a session of the Holston Conference at Lake Junaluska, NC, 76-year-old Bob Parrott, campus minister at the UTK Wesley Foundation for 29 years, received the Francis Asbury Award, presented by the Conference Board of Higher Education. The award read: *"The Francis Asbury Award for fostering United Methodist Ministries in Higher Education awarded to Rev. Robert Parrott of the Holston Annual Conference for Outstanding Leadership in Supporting, Strengthening, and Promoting the Church's Higher Education*

THE SHINING OF LIGHT: A HISTORY OF THE WESLEY FOUNDATION
AT THE UNIVERSITY OF TENNESSEE, 1922-2007

Ministries." The award recognized not only an individual but the strategic importance of Wesley Foundations on state-supported campuses, and the particular significance of the Wesley Foundation at the University of Tennessee, Knoxville.

5

Shortly before the beginning of the 2007-2008 academic year, Wesley Foundation residents met for a day's retreat. Jackson Culpepper, Rose Spurrier. Rebecca Hodges, Danielle Haiden, Jonathan Young and Matthew Young engaged in discussion of basic ministry issues, together with David Jackson, Brandon Wright (the Student Intern), and Heather Godsey. They worked on issues of spiritual formation and on the outlines of the Christian covenant into which they had entered. In considering their roles as persons who enact hospitality and care for others, they defined hospitality as a Christian discipline, and sought scriptural bases for it in the New Testament parables. They also discussed the boundaries which delimit hospitality. They discussed their service assignments, which were to include assistance with building maintenance, yard supervision, litter removal, recycling and kitchen management. They agreed on a statement about their corporate image: "Residents are the public face of the Wesley Foundation. Please be courteous, welcoming and hospitable as possible at all times. Please help one another, especially when others are away....Thank you for your devotion and care of our facility." These agreements and understandings have resulted, among many other efforts, in a building in fall 2007 which is spacious, orderly and welcoming, reflecting the light which had always shown from the campus ministry.

Among the students actively involved in the fall 2007 ministry were Jackson Culpepper, Brandon Wright, Rose Spurrier, Rebecca Hodges, Danielle Haiden, Matthew Wang, Jonathan Wang, Victor Foster, Tricia Goetzka, Margaret Kauchak, Alli

IN A NEW WORLD
(2002-2007)

Yilling, Anne Marie Sherman, Kate Phelps, Neeley Polka, Hunter Pavlik, Norman Rivera, Gregg Corlew, Jill Wilson, Neal Charlton, Rachel Lenhart, Tyler Peterson and Sarah Monday.

Wednesday night discussion group, 2007

During Fall Break 2007, nine Wesley Foundation students, together with other students from the Agricultural campus, Church Street United Methodist Church and Concord United Methodist Church completed a four day mission trip to the Mississippi Gulf Coast. As reported in the October 16 issue of *The Daily Beacon* by Hunter Pavlik, Sports Editor and an active Wesley Foundation participant, they worked on various roofing projects, first at Moss Point, 29 miles northeast of Biloxi, and then in the city of Biloxi, in the preparation work needed before new drywalls could be installed. "While helping rebuild these houses, the student volunteers also learned what some of the storm survivors went through. A neighbor in Biloxi showed students video footage she had filmed during the hurricane from another neighbor's porch a few hundred yards from the coast. She described how eight residents from a local apartment complex were stuck in the surging waves that came up the street. Six of them were pulled to

THE SHINING OF LIGHT: A HISTORY OF THE WESLEY FOUNDATION AT THE UNIVERSITY OF TENNESSEE, 1922-2007

safety.....The neighbor then pointed to the house next door, and described how she had found a body after the storm. She described the smell of decaying flesh and how she had to hold on to the body for days until the local coroner could get around to all the dead bodies." Jill Wilson, one of the Wesley Foundation participants, commented, "I felt I made a difference because I could see the progress being made."

On Wednesday, December 5, the traditional candle lighting service in the Chapel offered the Advent reminder of the presence of the grace of God. Once again, when candles were lighted in the apse niches and were shared by congregants in the pews, there was the shining of light.

A view of the new world into which the Wesley Foundation has moved was offered by campus minister David Jackson in a Holston Conference publication, *Clergy Connection* (Volume 7, #1, Winter 2007), in which he wrote: "We have been hearing a lot the last few years about the lack of young adults in our churches. Being in campus ministry, I have an interesting perspective from which to view this phenomenon. Looking one way, I can see youth moving out of local church and into college or vocations. Looking the other way, I see college graduates moving out into the world to make their way. What I often see is a fundamental disconnect between these energetic young college graduates and the churches they encounter.....We are living in a culture in which some are inside the walls of the church and many young adults are outside. We have tried to coax, cajole and call young adults in for years now; maybe it is time for us to go out. This will be incredibly threatening to us and our institutions, but Jesus did say that those '*...who wish to save their life will have to give it away,"* and maybe he wasn't talking just to individuals but to churches as well.

"Post-moderns like conversation, not proclamation. They no longer live in a world that believes in Truth. They live in a world that believes in truths, many truths, and they are going to look suspiciously on an institution that insists on proclaiming one Truth…..Our task, I believe, is to bring our Truth into conversation with their truths. If the conversation is all one-sided (accept our Truth!), the talk will not last long. However, if we can, with integrity and authenticity, enter into conversation, then young adults will come to see value and truth in the Truth we have to offer. Conversion may not be instantaneous in such a scenario, it may take many cups of coffee, but the conversion may be just as real (not a bad Wesleyan take on conversion, by the way)….It is not so much convincing others we are right as it is in questing for the Truth together, and that may involve opening our beliefs and opinions to scrutiny and reflection (scary stuff). But if the Truth is the Truth, we can find it together."

The light shines.

THE SHINING OF LIGHT: A HISTORY OF THE WESLEY FOUNDATION
AT THE UNIVERSITY OF TENNESSEE, 1922-2007

On Melrose Place

AFTERWORD

"Take The Light With You"

Functioning in the midst of a major state university whose chief task is to teach, promote learning and engage in scholarly research, the UTK Wesley Foundation has developed its own specialized purpose -- to be the Church, to grapple with theological and social issues, to interpret the meanings of discipleship, to provide opportunities for mission and to assist in understanding the wider world into which young adults proceed. By these endeavors, the Wesley Foundation adds its significant, vital component to the larger experience of a university education.

Since the earliest days of the Church, light and the giving of light have been crucial metaphors for the Christian life, and have long symbolized both faith and knowledge. Light and learning move along the same trajectory. In the elegant, incandescent language of the Gospel of John, Jesus identifies himself with light: *"I am the light of the world. Whoever follows me will never walk in darkness, but will have the light of life."* Through hardship and struggle, through failure and success, the Wesley Foundation has sought to share this light.

At Wesley Foundation worship, the congregational benediction first written in 1989 continues to be used. The first stanza, sung to a traditional Spanish melody (found in *The United Methodist Hymnal* #356, in the words "Pues Si Vivimos [When We Are Living]") is sung with musical accompaniment; the second stanza is sung *a capella,* and the shift from accompanied voices to the blend of four-part choral singing still offers to many worshipers a moment of rare transcendence. There is a beauty in the voices which warms the heart.

THE SHINING OF LIGHT: A HISTORY OF THE WESLEY FOUNDATION AT THE UNIVERSITY OF TENNESSEE, 1922-2007

Go forth in goodness, for in Christ is goodness.
Go forth in justice, it is of the Lord.
When we are loving, when we are giving,
We belong to God, we belong to God.
(*a capella*)
Go forth believing, go forth forgiving,
Go forth in courage, in the hands of God.
When we are loving, and are forgiving,
We belong to God, we belong to God.
We belong to God, we belong to God.

A third *a capella* stanza, written now to mark its eighty-five years of ministry, expresses the enduring presence of the Wesley Foundation as it moves into the future.

Take the light with you, for it lights the way,
Share the light always, it is of the Lord.
When we are loving, and are light-giving,
We belong to God, we belong to God.
We belong to God, we belong to God.

AFTERWORD

Light!

THE SHINING OF LIGHT: A HISTORY OF THE WESLEY FOUNDATION
AT THE UNIVERSITY OF TENNESSEE, 1922-2007

Godspell, 1980

SOURCES
Books

Allen, Donald R., compiler. *Knox-Stalgia.* Knoxville, Tennessee, 1999.
Brewster, Dan F., Freeman, G. Ross. *Higher Education In the Southeastern Jurisdiction of The United Methodist Church, 1784-1984.* Atlanta, Parthenon Press (The Southeastern Jurisdictional Conference Council on Ministries), 1984.
Burrow, J.A., editor. *The Holston Annual 1922: Official Record of the Holston Annual Conference, Methodist Episcopal Church, South, Ninety-Ninth Session, Bristol, Virginia.*
Creekmore, Betsey Beeler. *Knoxville.* Third edition. Knoxville, University of Tennesee Press, 1976.
Creekmore, Betsey Beeler. *Knox County, Tennessee: A History in Pictures.* Norfolk-Virginia Beach, The Downing Company Publishers, 1988.
Creekmore, Betsey B., text; Baumann, J. Bruce, editor, designer. *200 Tennessee: A Celebration of 200 Years of the University.* Scripps-Howard Publishing, Inc., 1994.
Fuller, Edmund. *The Christian Idea of Education.* New Haven, Connecticut, Yale University Press, 1957.
Gibson, Samuel Norris. *A Study of the Wesley Foundations and the Campus Ministry of the Methodist Church: A National Study of the Campus Ministry of the Methodist Church in Tax-Supported and Independent Colleges and Universities.* Nashville, Tennessee, The Division of Higher Education, General Board of Education of the Methodist Church, 1967.
Grupo go Trbajo Numero 5, Junio-Sjulio, 1980; Santiago, Samuel Lopez, asistent linguistico. *?Nchi Tsini Nuhu Saha Cruee Mee Ta Nchaan Gaa Catsi Cuee Mee Cuee Cuichi?* Knoxville, Tennessee, UTK Wesley Foundation, 1980.
McNabb, William Ross. *Tradition, Innovation and Romantic Images: The Architecture of Historic Knoxville.* Knoxville, Frank H. McClung Museum, The University of Tennessee Knoxville, 1991.

Ministry on Campus: A United Methodist Mission Statement and Survey Report. Nashville, Tennessee, National Committee on UMHE, 1977.

THE SHINING OF LIGHT: A HISTORY OF THE WESLEY FOUNDATION AT THE UNIVERSITY OF TENNESSEE, 1922-2007

Montgomery, James Riley, Folmsbee, Samuel J., Green, Lee Seifert. *To Foster Knowledge: A History of the University of Tennessee, 1794-1970.* Knoxville, The University of Tennessee Press, 1974.

Platt, S. Joseph, editor. *A Book of Remembrance: Church Street United Methodist Church (1793-1816?)-1975.* Knoxville, Tennessee, 1982.

Shockley, Donald G. *Campus Ministry: The Church Beyond Itself.* Louisville, Kentucky. John Knox Press/Westminster, 1989.

Spores, Ronald. *The Mixtec Kings and Their People.* Norman, Oklahoma, The University of Oklahoma Press, 1967.

Zimmerman, Elena Irish. *Knoxville: A Postcard Memoir, 1900-1930.* Knoxville, East Tennessee Historical Society, 1991.

Church Street United Methodist Church Archives

The Wesley Foundation, The University of Tennessee: The Founding of the Methodist Student Center. Recollections by Ruth and Frank DeFriese. Unpublished manuscript. 1993.

Articles

Jackson, David. "The Post-Modern Pastor," *Clergy Connection: Holston Conference of the United Methodist Church.* Volume 7, Number 1, Winter 2007, p. 3.

O'Steen, Neal. "How the YMCA Saved A Godless Institution: Or Why the Y Became a Tradition on the Hill," *The Tennessee Alumnus.* Winter 1986, pp.31-34.

Files/Newspapers/Public Records

Records/Minutes of the Student Council/Coordinating Cabinet, UTK Wesley Foundation
Records of Publications, UTK Wesley Foundation
Annual Reports, Campus Minister, UTK Wesley Foundation
Individual Project Reports, *Operation Mixtec I & II*
Records/Minutes of the Board of Directors, UTK Wesley Foundation
Knoxville, Tennessee City Directories
The Knoxville Journal archives